Management Accounting in Practice

by

J B Coates

C P Rickwood

R J Stacey

The Chartered Institute of Management Accountants
63 Portland Place
London W1N 4AB

First published in 1991, revised 1995 by:
The Chartered Institute of Management Accountants

ISBN 1 874784 36 1

The publishers of this book consider that it is a worthwhile contribution to discussion, without necessarily sharing the views expressed, which are those of the authors.

No responsibility for loss occasioned to any person acting or refraining from action as a result of any material in this publication can be accepted by the authors or publishers.

Contents

Acknowledgements

The authors gratefully acknowledge the support given by the ESRC in the preparation of these Case Studies.

They also wish to express their thanks for the time and help given by the managers and accountants of the companies visited in providing the information on which the studies are based.

Permission has been granted by Academic Press Ltd, Harcourt Brace Jovanovich Publishers to include the following paper, which was previously published in *Management Accounting Research* Vol. 1 No. 1 March 1990.

Stapylton: Strategic management accounting to gain competitive advantage.

1 Introduction

There exists an array of techniques which the management accountant can draw upon in fulfilling the special role of providing that management information which facilitates the planning, decision-making and control activities of the business organisation. The majority of these techniques are far from new. Indeed, *Professor Kaplan*[1] has suggested that most were known and in use in the first quarter of the 20th century. However, mere proficiency with the technical operation even of updated versions of 60-year-old methods is not a sufficient basis for maintaining the management accountant's much sought-after role. A key factor is the expertise which is required in the selection of the methods appropriate to the context in which it is to operate, and in the implementation of the chosen method in its particular application.

Whilst financial accounting may be governed by restrictions from the law, accounting standards and other sources, management accounting offers an unfettered choice. Indeed, it may well be the exercise of this choice that gives one organisation the relative advantage over its competitors that leads to its own successful performance.

Consistent with this is the view that management accounting should not be directed only at a company's internal functioning, but should also recognise its external environment. *Bromwich and Bhimani*[2] argue that 'there is a need for management accounting to become more externally focused to enable the enterprise to look outwards to the final goods market'.

They advocate the adoption of strategic management accounting which adopts a long-term horizon taking into account external information including, for example, 'enterprise costs relative to its competitors'.

There have been pleas for more research effort to be put into the investigation of how management accounting operates in context,[3] and there has been some response to this.[4] In developing the skill in application of the expert, both the student and the practising management accountant may have much to gain by examining the experiences of a range of companies. The case studies presented in this book represent a contribution to this.

1.1 Structure and use of cases

Several features of the structure of the cases have been provided to help in using them within courses.

In addition to the descriptions given later in this introduction, each case commences with a synopsis. This is intended not only to give an overview which will aid in focusing on the case's main features, but also in the selection of cases to co-ordinate with the development and emphasis of each particular course.

Each case adopts the same structure, providing background information in the section immediately following the synopsis. Early awareness of the situation of the case is important to promote the relationship of management accounting within its context.

The case details which represent the major part of each study contain little in the way of interpretations and commentary. The readers are encouraged to consider for themselves the implications of the companies' procedures, policies and responses.

Where appropriate, interpretations and comment are postponed for inclusion in concluding remarks. These are offered with the intention of setting out the reflections of the company or the authors on the situation.

The cases are not intended to present problem situations in search of a solution to be provided by the student. Instead, they include both the situation and the solutions that have been adopted in actual companies. However, their role in the teaching and learning frame of reference is boosted by discussion in which the student plays a substantial part. Each case could be followed simply by the instruction 'Discuss'. In this volume, the cases are accompanied by a series of questions aimed at invoking more specific responses to the invitation to discuss and to direct attention either to particular parts of the case or to relevant broader considerations. The student is encouraged to draw upon knowledge of the fundamental techniques of management accounting.

1.2 Source of cases

Each case represents the result of a study by the authors of real companies[5] and their actual responses to the situations they faced. Each may offer some insight into how management accounting may be applied. Investigations involved a series of interviews conducted by more than one team member. Write-ups have been sent to interviewees, principally to verify content and identify omissions.

This response from interviewees was also an essential step in overcoming a major barrier to the potential observer of practice – that of confidentiality. The desire of companies to remain anonymous and not be identified with the management accounting approaches it has used may be an indication of the value of the skills that have been discussed. It means that the cases are masked so that the familiar and identifiable names of companies have been replaced by false names and, in some instances, products have been changed, although substantial efforts have been made to ensure that the industry setting is comparable. All the companies were operating in the UK as members of well-known corporate groups.

1.3 Relevant scope of management accounting

Just as the manner in which management accountants may perform their function can be expected to differ between organisations, the responsibilities they are assigned are also likely to show substantial diversity. In a competitive environment, companies will aim to design their organisation in the manner which they consider most advantageous. No structure is accepted as universally optimal. Systems and job definitions vary. However, the responsibilities of the management accountant are likely to be made up of the following:

- the design of management accounting systems;
- the selection and implementation of systems for cost collection and allocation which support chosen approaches to costing reflecting, inter alia, views on cost behaviour and performance responsibility;
- the creation, collection and analysis of data handled by these systems;
- the presentation and communication of selected information to other managers for planning, control and decision-making purposes.

The focus of the cases in this book is on two broad areas, *viz.*, the operation for control purposes of performance measurement in divisionalised companies; and analysis of cost behaviour where particular attention has been given to the impact of context.

In three out of the four cases concerned with divisional control, transfer pricing methods are significant. Transfer pricing is a topic capable of generating considerable interest, not least because of the variety of technical methods put forward in texts. For some time now, it has been recognised that the selection of a transfer pricing method could not be based on a narrow view of optimality.[6] Transfer pricing should not be seen as an end in itself, but is to be selected for its compatibility with overriding corporate goals. It is capable of fulfilling two functions which may not always be mutually consistent – namely, integrating and co-ordinating divisional activity, on the one hand, whilst, on the other, permitting some autonomy and independence of decision-making in separate divisions.

The trade-off between these two functions is made complex by the uncertainty of change in the environment and by the different access to information. *Kaplan*[7] draws attention to the resulting difficulty: 'Under conditions that make decentralisation worthwhile – that is, an uncertain environment with private information possessed by local managers – we do not know a great deal about optimal transfer pricing.' Divisional control will face at least as much difficulty from these conditions, and the observations of practice in this book shed further light on the 'private information' and the information monopolies it creates.

The practice of cost behaviour analysis appears to have suffered some neglect by researchers. *Kaplan*[8] examined management accounting papers published in academic journals in the period 1926–83. He found just 31 field studies out of 642 articles. Only eight of these were not directed at budgetary control and performance evaluation. None gave attention to cost behaviour, cost allocation or cost accounting.

Much of the field of management accounting has grown out of cost accounting. Indeed, a number of writers[9] have suggested that excessive devotion to the costing needs of the financial accountant may have unduly distorted management accounting and hampered its development. Although cost information used in financial accounting may be a cheap, secondhand source, it is likely to be inappropriate.

Cost is a term used probably as widely as any other word in accounting. Whilst financial accounting requirements may have focused on transaction-based historic cost, the range of uses to which the term is applied is not satisfied by a single approach to measurement.

Decision-making applications have emphasised the relevance of those costs which change. In turn, this has seen concentration in management accounting on the analysis of cost into fixed and variable components. Where cost behaviour is observed in the studies in this book the simple fixed/variable classification seems insufficient to describe the approach adopted. Cost changes do not usefully fit the alternate description of being either fixed and therefore constant when volume changes, or variable such that increases in volume automatically results in increased cost. This dependent relationship appears to be an oversimplification of the determination of cost. In particular, it excludes the all-important role of managers in setting cost levels.

Examination of procedures in their context may help in recognising that management accounting is not an end in itself. It is part of the total management process and the accountant is one of the managers whose position is maintained and function is met by using special access to financial data and skills in its interpretation and analysis. Management accounting can be observed as a practical exercise; its tools are imprecise and must be applied in the face of imperfect knowledge, disparate goals, and problems of control and co-ordination within the organisation.

1.4 *Summary of case contents*

Solent

Faced with a requirement to improve its return on investment, this company examined how performance would be affected by a set of possible options to shut down part or all of the operations in its divisions. The case highlights the conflict between the information used for measuring divisional performance and that appropriate to decision-making.

Central Freight

This case is concerned with the decision to change divisional organisation and performance measurement from that based on investment centres to a budgeted profit centre basis. The impact on the application of the transfer pricing scheme is examined. An explanation of the reasons for the change is given in an excerpt from an interview with the Finance Director.

Belcom

Transfer pricing in Belcom is based on the Group's policy for the calculation of standard product costs. Their treatment of direct, indirect and overhead costs is described, and details from the company's procedures manual and budgets are made available. These enable some assessment to be made of the effectiveness of the approach in the face of inter-divisional rivalry.

Kimco

This case describes the methods of divisional control employed in a conglomerate group. The group's normal business activity involves regular acquisition and disposal of subsidiaries, and their success depends, in part, on being able to cope with these changes in composition smoothly while motivating and controlling subsidiaries to produce good performance. The resulting design of the transfer pricing system encourages autonomy, and it is the internal audit function which adds a key ingredient to performance control.

Carcomp

This is the first of the cases in which divisional performance is not a significant concern. It is concerned with the assessment of product profitability which is seen to fluctuate over time. These variations are not due to any particular change in the product itself but due to changes elsewhere in the company. Indeed, the case shows how information used during a period when the product was considered unviable forms the basic data for a decision to reacquire the product line. The approach to data collection in the face of an urgent decision is set out.

Eastcote

This case adds to the recognition that cost is dependent upon context. It may be rare, in that it considers service costs as an interesting illustration of the impact of declining marginal costs on product portfolios. Building on the basic technique of breakeven analysis, it describes a company recognising the importance of the time horizon on the response in cost that can occur (or be made to occur) when volume is changed.

Midlands Metals

The approach to classifying costs as fixed or variable is determined, in this company, not so much by any in-built nature of the costs' dependence on volume, as by the management purpose it may serve. In this case, the circumstances in which management can turn discretionary labour costs into committed costs is explored. It can provide an introduction to identifying those costs which can be 'managed' to be in line with anticipated levels of business. Control is directed at those responsible for such managed costs.

Stapylton A

As in Midland Metals, attention is directed at those costs which are managed – where management must decide their level at the start of the planning period to match them to the underlying level of business. The control system adopted is based on directing accountability to those responsible for setting cost levels. This, in turn, is partly dependent on the time horizon within which managers are allowed to make decisions. The resulting hierarchical control of overhead costs reduces dependence on cost apportionment.

Stapylton B

Although this is a self-contained case, it can be viewed as an extension of the preceding case. It examines the manner in which a management team responds to a competitive threat, but highlights the special role played by the management accountants. Information is gathered relating not only to internal costs and revenues but to those of rivals as well. The management accountant uses his 'information monopoly' to gain access to other 'private data' – the perceptions and knowledge of the marketing staff. In addition to arriving at a decision, control mechanisms are created simultaneously.

Edford

This examines the decision by a company to begin adopting an activity based costing (ABC) approach. It describes the existing costing system and identifies some of the major reasons for dissatisfaction with it. A partial approach to ABC is selected and this warrants discussion. How the company investigates the potential for ABC is set out, together with the studies it undertakes in preparing for implementation.

Gatwick Components

This case is set within a multinational product division of a large group. In particular, it recounts the situation where the transfer price between two operating units is imposed to produce desired motivational behaviour. The case allows a number of varied facets of management to be explored: organisation structures, transfer pricing, performance measurement, sales management control/performance measurement, inter-unit comparison and the behavioural effects of these decisions, all within a multinational trading environment.

Notes

1 Kaplan, R S, 'Measuring Manufacturing Performance: A New Challenge for Management Accounting Reserved', *Accounting Review*, October 1983.

2 Bromwich, M and Bhimani, A, *Management Accounting: Evolution not Revolution*, CIMA 1989.

3 See, for example, Hopwood, A, 'On Trying to Study Accounting in the Context in which it Operates', *Accounting, Organisations and Society,* No. 2/3, 1983 and Kaplan, R S, 'The Case for Case Studies in Management Accounting Research', paper presented at American Accounting Association Annual Conference, 1984, and Tomkins, C and Groves, R E V, 'The Everyday Accountant and Researching his Reality', *Accounting, Organisations and Society*, Vol. 8, No. 4, 1983.

4 Roberts, J and Scapens, R, 'Accounting Systems and Systems of Accountability – Understanding Accounting Practices in their Organisational Contexts', *Accounting, Organisations and Society*, Vol. 10, No. 4, 1985.

5 The case study research embodied in all but the last two cases in this volume was made possible through funds made available by the Economic and Social Research Council. The authors gratefully acknowledge their support.

6 Watson, D H S and Baumler, J V, 'Transfer Pricing: A Behavioural Context', *The Accounting Review*, Vol. L, No. 3, July 1975.

7 Kaplan, R S (1983), *op.cit.*

8 Kaplan, R S (1984), *op.cit.*

9 See Cooper, R, 'You need a new cost system when . . . ', *Harvard Business Review*, Jan/Feb. 1989.

Johnson, H J and Kaplan, R S, *Relevance Lost: The Rise and Fall of Management Accounting*, Boston, Mass., Harvard Business School Press, 1987.

Cooper, R and Kaplan, R S, 'How Cost Accounting Systematically Distorts Product Costs', in Bruns, W J and Kaplan, R S (eds), *Accounting and Management: Field Study Perspectives*, Harvard Business School Press, 1987.

2 Solent

2.1 Synopsis

This case is concerned with a shut-down decision, but one in which investment centre performance measurement played an important but inconsistent role. It illustrates how a particular operating company within a group was required to pursue performance targets dominated by the return on assets measure. In responding to demands from the group for improved results from the operating company, in both return on assets and profit margin, operating company management did not rely on their existing management controls for the separate locations they managed. Instead they considered alternative scenarios, calculating for each option the total operating results using group measurement bases. These bases were dependent upon accounting conventions, not necessarily appropriate for good economic decision-making.

The case presents the necessary background and detailed summaries of the data upon which the decision was made, and points to the conflict of this decision with indications of existing performance provided in the routine management control reports.

It offers case study evidence which can support the examination of a number of management accounting considerations. These include performance measurement for the evaluation of investment and profit centres; the identification of sets of decision alternatives; the collection and presentation of relevant cost and revenue data for special decisions; the potential conflict between specified performance targets and good decision-making and the consequent behavioural implications.

2.2 Background

The company

Solent Ltd is a wholly owned subsidiary of a large multinational and forms, by itself, a division of the group. Solent markets a range of products in the paper industry, supplying consumer products to pharmaceutical chains and supermarkets.

In the middle of the 1980/81 financial year the group main board became concerned about the performance of Solent Ltd, and as a result the group board set certain targets for Solent to achieve over the next five years. These were:

(i) An increase in their primary measure of performance, return on operating assets, to 25 per cent per annum before company taxation, to be achieved within the five-year time span;
(ii) A positive cash flow in each year;
(iii) Improvement in the divisional profit-to-sales margin to 12½ per cent over the same period.

The division operated from two separate sites at either end of the country. The older site was in Southampton where a single product range, tissues, was made. The second site, Newcastle, was considerably larger and was responsible for producing a full range of products including one line in the tissue range, namely tissue handkerchiefs; its output represented a sales value of about 1½ times that of Southampton.

Production at the newer site in the North-east was analysed into three groups in connection with the considerations which subsequently ensued. These three groups were major products, tissues and minor products, representing about 68 per cent, 18 per cent and 14 per cent respectively of the sales volume of this site. The tissue handkerchief line used the same basic bought-in material as that made at Southampton, although the final product was packaged in a substantially different manner.

On receiving the targets from the group board, the divisional board of Solent decided to set up a working party drawing on management accounting staff, production management and union representatives from both sites. Its task was to identify a set of alternative policies designed to meet the main board requirements and to carry out an evaluation recommending a chosen option. The working party was set up in February 1981 and was required to report before the end of the financial year on the following 30 June.

The working party was given considerable scope and authority. It was made clear that it should review the merits and production basis of both tissues and minor products, but that major product activities were to continue unchanged in the North-east. The working party was given authority to examine costs and production methods at both sites and to have access to any relevant information available within Solent. In addition, it was given a small budget which could be used to obtain market information concerning the products.

2.3 *Case details*

The search for a response

The working party initially identified two broad approaches which might be utilised to meet the required objectives. These were either to increase output and sales in order to improve the utilisation of existing facilities, or to achieve reductions in costs. The latter might be achieved with no modification of product ranges or plant. Additionally, alternatives which involved asset reduction were considered.

Initial emphasis was directed at opportunities for increasing volume, a positive response which would be attractive both to employees and management. Solent's own marketing function was asked to prepare projections of the market in each of the twelve product ranges which the company produced. These projections showed forecasts of the total volume for each product and of the market share which Solent products were expected to achieve. Following a period of decline in market share in most of the products, the marketing projections were not very encouraging. No growth in physical volume was anticipated even though this represented an improvement in market share for all but one of the product ranges. The possibility of substantial volume expansion was considered attainable only if associated with a substantial addition to media expenditure. At this stage such a proposal was not considered feasible in the light of the recent difficulties faced by the group. Consequently the use of expansion to meet the required objectives was rejected.

The division had already prepared a five-year plan using marketing forecasts which suggested that the return on operating assets was expected to increase from 15½ per cent to 17½ per cent over the five-year horizon (see Table B). This increase is due mainly to sales value growth exceeding increases in overhead costs and, to a lesser extent, asset expansion. Overhead and asset increases were expected to be within a range of 5–7 per cent.

The planning activities of the working party continued by revising the data in the long-range plan to compute the cost savings required to produce the required return on assets of 25 per cent at the end of five years. They found that this would require reductions over five years in direct cost of sales of some 3½ per cent but in overheads of just over 10 per cent (see Table C). Savings in direct cost of sales would be difficult to achieve as this cost was mainly bought-in materials. It was considered that the likelihood of identifying ways in which further savings of this order could be made was small and that, given the urgency of a need to identify a suitable policy, it would be advisable to consider other options as well as, if not instead of, the suggestion of reducing costs. The working party members were satisfied that they had given the attention to cost reduction that this brief demanded but that their efforts would be more effective in other directions.

Establishing alternatives

The working party then turned their attention to options which would help to boost the percentage returns by achieving a reduction in the operating assets themselves. Since major product activities were to continue at the Newcastle site in the North-east, their focus was on options involving changes in tissue and minor product activities.

One of these options was the abandonment of the original home of Solent, Southampton, as the main source of tissue output. Initially, it might have been considered that this option was not worth further attention since the existing performance of this site appeared to be very good. In fact, the site's own return on assets of 31½ per cent was well in excess of the target of 25 per cent and the tissue range was one of the most successful of the Solent products, generating some two-thirds of the total profit of the division while representing about 40 per cent of divisional turnover.

By contrast, the performance measures for the minor products range appeared particularly poor. The sales margins on this range were computed to be less than 2 per cent and the return on assets figure produced a figure of little over 2½ per cent. In Table A the budget for each type is shown, using the approach adopted for internal reporting to the Solent board. The operating assets attributed to each group of projects include some which are specific to the products, including stocks, debtors less creditors and most of the plant and machinery. However, land and buildings and some machinery at Newcastle represent shared facilities; their values are apportioned to products on various basis with land and buildings apportioned on the basis of weight of output.

The options considered represented different locations of tissue output between the two sites in combination with continuing or discounting the minor product work. Five options were identified. These were:

(i) Minor products to be discontinued, but with no other changes in major products, and tissue handkerchiefs to continue to be produced at Newcastle, Southampton to continue its present tissue production.
(ii) All tissues, including tissue handkerchiefs, to be produced at Southampton, with Newcastle to continue dealing with all other products, major and minor.
(iii) As in (ii) above, tissue handkerchiefs, to be transferred to Southampton, but in addition Newcastle to cease production of minor products.
(iv) Southampton to be closed and all products to be produced at Newcastle, including the full range of tissues transferred from Southampton.
(v) As in (iv) above but, in addition, production of minor products to cease so Newcastle to produce major products and all tissues.

All these options were to be compared with the existing situation presented in Table A. Taken together with the situation of 'no change', six possible site activity options were identified.

Data generation and evaluation

The working party carried out the collection and presentation of data to identify the financial implications of each alternative both in terms of the one-off effects and the recurrent effects. Its evaluations are summarised in Table D, and details for each of these options are presented in Tables E to I.

One-off effects

In carrying out the calculations a number of one-off financial changes were quantified; these are summarised in Table D(b). In addition to the cash outlay of £15,000 required to transfer tissue handkerchief production to Southampton, plant at Newcastle with a book value of £406,000 would be written off. A further write-off of £493,000 would result from abandoning minor products. The option of transferring tissues to Newcastle would involve writing off plant of £1,032,000. The cash costs of some £130,000 of transferring tissues to Newcastle would be more than offset by the availability of a regional development grant of £254,000.

The sale of the Southampton factory would realise some £1.85m against a net book value at the end of 1979/80 of £2.82m. By way of comparison, the realisable value of the Newcastle factory was set at some £3½m against a net book value of just over £13m. However, it was unlikely that such a realisation would be achieved given the present state of industrial activity in the North-east and, if major product activity was to continue, this would not be possible, although it may have proved possible to rent out some of the space released. Table D also shows the cost to the division of redundancy payments. However, the working party also expressed concern for the social impact of the redundancies. It was these considerations that had been fundamental to the requirement to continue major product activity at Newcastle.

Recurrent effects

Evaluation of the various options was made for the next financial year, 1981/82, principally in terms of the primary measure of performance, return on operating assets, with sales margins being calculated as an additional statistic . The anticipated effects of each of the options can be identified by comparing each of the Tables E to I with the original budget set out in Table A. Measurement of assets and of revenue, income and expenditure items was established using the same accounting policies employed for internal financial reporting, essentially a historic cost approach with site overheads apportioned to all products, but with no apportionments between sites. However, for the purposes of this evaluation, attention was focused on overhead changes with no attempt to associate these with product lines within a site. A similar approach was adopted for operating assets, that is changes affecting more than one line are shown on a site basis only.

Table E shows that adoption of the first option eliminates all sales revenue and direct costs associated with the minor products. In addition, an annual saving of overheads of nearly a quarter of a million pounds is estimated for the first year. Included is a reduction in depreciation charge due to plant and machinery eliminations. In addition to these plant reductions, all current assets arising from minor product business would be realised. This is reflected in return calculations but, consistent with the company's reporting approach, no one-off effect is shown.

For the options involving the transferring of special tissues to Southampton (Tables F and G), although a number of overhead costs formerly met at Newcastle would move with the production activity, a net saving in operating costs of over £300,000 would result. Some plant and machinery would also be transferred and a small part of these costs was regarded as capital. Although debtors net of creditors would be unchanged by bringing the two tissue products together, there would be a significant reduction in stock levels.

The closure of a complete site under either of the final options has the most far-reaching implications for overhead levels (Tables H and I). Many service functions existed at both sites, and the cost of expansion in capacity required at Newcastle would be significantly less than the costs of running the separate facility in Southampton. Although small, canteen and cleaning costs provide good illustrations of this; one can readily accept that the additional facilities and staff to meet the needs of an expanded labour force would cost substantially less than the cost of an independent service. In addition, there would be very large savings in maintenance, rates and establishment costs. Some reduction in transport costs were anticipated from the gathering together of the division's activities.

Reference is also appropriate to the operating asset effects. The land and building would be completely eliminated from the return on asset ratio calculation. In addition, plant needs in the new location would be more compatible with current levels and modes of activity, permitting further eliminations.

2.4 *Concluding remarks*

The decision

Comparison of the options in the summary (Table D) enabled the working party to recommend the closure of the Southampton site but retention of the full product range. Although this did not immediately achieve the required targets, it was asserted (but not calculated) that the forecast changes in costs and revenues in the long-range plan would produce the desired results.

Not surprisingly, there was considerable dissatisfaction with this recommendation from all members associated with the Southampton site. Their feelings were strengthened by the knowledge that the performance of this site was both well above the target and considerably better than either of the other products' groups. Nevertheless, the recommendation was accepted and implemented.

2.5 *Questions*

1. Consider the choice of divisional performance measurement applied by the group to Solent and its implications for internal control.

2. Identify the impact of accounting conventions on divisional performance measurement. Examine the arguments for and against the use of measures which are compatible with those used for financial accounting purposes.

3. Assess the manner in which the working party searched for a solution to the problem faced by Solent and their identification of options for detailed consideration.

4. Discuss the working party's approach to evaluating the options, giving attention to:

   (i) the items included as one-off effects;
   (ii) the effects on revenues and costs of sales;
   (iii) the effects on overheads;
   (iv) the criteria used for selecting a recommended alternative.

   What other approaches might have been usefully considered for each of the above evaluations?

5. Within the limits of the information available, evaluate the impact of the options on the results of Solent from the point of view of the group.

6. (a) What decision would the routine ROI information given in the Budget (Table A) suggest? Explain why the working party came to an entirely different decision.

   (b) What are the implications of the case and the discussion in part (a) on the use of return on investment for management decision-making? Give attention to abandonment/shutdown decisions.

   (c) Consider the potential conflicts highlighted in part (a) for the management of human assets.

2.6 *Appendix*

Table A

Solent Ltd – Budget for 12 months to 30 June 1992

	Newcastle					
	Major Products £000	*Tissue Hankies £000*	*Minor Products £000*	*Total Newcastle £000*	*S'ton Tissues £000*	*Division Total £000*
Sales	19,376	5,127	4,008	28,511	18,987	47,498
Cost of sales (=Direct cost)	13,842	3,660	3,123	20,625	11,899	32,524
Overheads	4,089	1,012	807	5,908	4,465	10,373
Total cost	17,931	4,672	3,930	26,533	16,364	42,897
Profit	1,445	455	78	1,978	2,623	4,601
Sales margin %	7.5	8.9	1.9	6.9	13.8	9.7
Operating assets						
Stocks	2,513	692	433	3,638	2,528	6,166
Debtors less creditors	420	104	95	619	392	1,011
Plant and machinery	2,702	669	554	3,925	2,588	6,513
Land and buildings	9,104	2,252	1,798	13,154	2,820	15,974
Total assets	14,739	3,717	2,880	21,336	8,328	29,664
Return on operating assets %	9.8	12.2	2.7	9.3	31.5	15.5

Table B

Solent Ltd – Long-range plan

	1981/82	*1982/83*	*1983/84*	*1984/85*	*1985/86*
	£000	*£000*	*£000*	*£000*	*£000*
Sales value	47,498	50,580	53,960	57,400	61,500
Cost of sales (Direct)	32,524	34,520	36,870	39,300	41,920
Overhead	10,374	11,105	11,620	12,120	12,950
Total cost	42,897	45,625	48,490	51,420	54,870
Profit	4,601	4,995	5,470	5,980	6,630
Sales margin %	9.7	9.8	10.1	10.4	10.8
Total assets	29,664	31,138	34,160	35,390	37,690
Return on assets %	15.5	15.9	16.0	16.9	17.6

Table C

Solent Ltd – Long-range plan

	1985/86	
	£000	*£000*
Sales		61,500
Operating assets	37,690	
Required profit to give a return of 25%		9,422
Target costs		52,078
Cost of sales @ 96.5% of 41,920		40,453
Maximum overhead		11,625

Required overhead saving = 12,950 – 11,625
= 1,325 i.e. 10.2%

Table D

(a) Summary of options for production

	Lost Sales £000	Cost Savings £000	Profit £000	Margin %	Assets £000	Return %
Existing	–	–	4,601	9.7	29,664	15.5
Option 1	(4,008)	3,372	3,965	9.1	28,643	13.8
Option 2	–	317	4,918	10.4	28,994	17.0
Option 3	(4,008)	3,689	4,282	9.8	27,973	15.3
Option 4	–	1,045	5,646	11.9	25,548	22.1
Option 5	(4,008)	4,417	5,010	11.5	24,527	20.4

(b) Summary of one-off costs and benefits (£000s)

	Plant Relocation	Govt Grants	Redundancy Costs	Plant Write-off	Property Disposal Sale Proceeds	Property Disposal NBV Write-off	Total
Option 1	–	–	103	493	–	–	596
Option 2	15	–	71	406	–	–	492
Option 3	15	–	174	899	–	–	1,088
Option 4	130	(254)	182	1,032	(1,850)	2,820	2,060
Option 5	130	(254)	182	1,525	(1,850)	2,820	2,553

Table E

Budget for Option 1: Minor products discontinued at Newcastle, Southampton unchanged

	Newcastle				
	Major Products	*Tissue Hankies*	*Total Newcastle*	*S'ton Tissues*	*Division Total*
	£000	*£000*	*£000*	*£000*	*£000*
Sales	19,376	5,127	24,503	18,987	43,490
Cost of sales	13,842	3,660	17,505	11,899	29,401
Overheads			5,659	4,465	10,124
Total cost			23,161	16,364	39,525
Profit			1,342	2,623	3,965
Sales margin %			5.5	13.8	9.1
Operating Assets					
Stocks	2,513	692	3,205	2,528	5,733
Debtors less creditors	420	104	524	392	916
Plant and machinery			3,432	2,588	6,020
Land and buildings			13,154	2,820	15,974
Total assets			20,315	8,328	28,643
Return on assets %			6.6	31.5	13.8

Discontinued minor products – schedule of overhead savings

	£000
Factory management	82
Maintenance	41
Stores	36
Inspection	24
Insurance	9
Heat, light, water	15
Depreciation	42
	249

Table F

Budget for Option 2: Tissue handkerchiefs transferred from Newcastle to Southampton. Newcastle continues to produce major and minor products, Southampton produces existing tissue range plus tissue handkerchiefs.

	Major Products £000	*Tissue Hankies £000*	*Minor Products £000*	*Total Newcastle £000*	*S'ton Tissues £000*	*Division Total £000*
Sales		19,376	4,008	23,384	24,114	47,498
Cost of sales		13,842	3,123	16,965	15,559	32,524
Overheads				5,134	4,922	10,056
Total cost				22,099	20,481	42,580
Profit				1,285	3,633	4,918
Sales margin %				5.5	15.1	10.4
Stocks		2,513	433	2,946	2,952	5,898
Debtors less creditors		420	95	515	496	1,011
Plant and machinery				3,339	2,772	6,111
Land and buildings				13,154	2,820	15,974
Total assets				19,954	9,040	28,994
Return on assets %				6.4	40.2	17.0

Transfer to Southampton – schedule of overhead savings/costs

	Savings: Newcastle £000	*Cost increases: Southampton £000*
Factory management	227	115
Manufacturing control	181	176
Maintenance	135	42
Stores	82	25
Inspection	47	45
Insurance	13	18
Heat, light, water	22	17
Telephone	9	9
Depreciation	58	10
	774	457

Net savings £317,000

Table G

Budget for Option 3: Tissue handkerchiefs transferred to Southampton and minor products discontinued so that Newcastle produces major products only. Southampton produces all tissue handkerchiefs.

	Newcastle Major Products £000	*S'ton All tissues £000*	*Division £000*
Sales	19,376	24,114	43,490
Cost of sales	13,842	15,559	29,401
Overhead	4,885	4,922	9,807
Total cost	18,727	20,481	39,208
Profit	649	3,633	4,282
Sales margin %	3.3	15.1	9.8
Operating Assets			
Stocks	2,513	2,952	5,465
Debtors less creditors	420	492	916
Plant and machinery	2,846	2,772	5,618
Land and buildings	13,154	2,820	15,974
Total assets	18,933	9,040	27,973
Return on assets %	3.4	40.2	15.3

Table H

Budget for Option 4: Southampton is closed and production transferred to Newcastle. Newcastle produces major products, all tissues and minor products.

	Major Products £000	*Tissue Hankies £000*	*Minor Products £000*	*Division (All Newcastle) Total £000*
Sales	19,376	24,114	4,008	47,498
Cost of sales	13,842	15,559	3,123	32,524
Overheads				9,328
Total cost				41,852
Profit				5,646
Sales margin %				11.9

Operating Assets

	Existing Newcastle £000	*Additional Newcastle £000*	*Division Total £000*
Stocks	3,638	2,260	5,898
Debtors less creditors	619	392	1,011
Plant and machinery	3,925	1,560	5,485
Land and buildings	13,154	–	13,154
Total assets	21,336	4,212	25,548
Return on operating assets %			22.1

Transfer to Newcastle – schedule of overhead savings

	£000
Factory management	123
Maintenance	215
Stores	98
Inspection	63
Personnel	81
Cleaning	10
Insurance	29
Accounts	13
Canteen	39
Heat, light, water, telephone	28
Rates, establishment costs	234
Depreciation	113
	1,026
Distribution	19
	1,045

Table I

Budget for Option 3: Southampton is closed and production transferred to Newcastle. Newcastle ceases minor product activity and produces major products plus all tissues.

	Major Products	*Tissues*	*Division (All Newcastle) Total*
	£000	*£000*	*£000*
Sales	19,376	24,114	43,490
Cost of sales	13,842	15,559	29,401
Overheads			9,079
Total cost			38,480
Profit			5,010
Sales margin %			11.5
Operating Assets			
Stocks	2,513	2,952	5,465
Debtors less creditors	420	496	916
Plant and machinery			4,992
Land and buildings			13,154
Total assets			24,527
Return on assets %			20.4

3
Central Freight

3.1 Synopsis

This study is concerned with the changes made in the performance measurement systems of a large transport business (Central Freight), from a budgeted investment centre basis to that of budgeted profit centres, the reasons for the change and the impacts of inter-company transactions and transfer pricing policies.

Part A concentrates on the budgeted investment centre approach originally adopted by Central Freight in circumstances where significant proportions of the revenues and costs of some product and profit centres were affected by inter-company trading requirements and transfer pricing policies.

Part B considers the introduction of a budgeted profit centre approach, established to reflect changing organisational and financial circumstances and intended to remove some perceived deficiencies of the previous system – though arguably introducing others. The inter-company trading and transfer pricing policies remained the same under both systems.

Part C consists of an excerpt of the more salient points from an interview with the Financial Director regarding corporate policies, attention extending to the principles, reasons and purposes behind the change to the current profit centre approach.

3.2 Background

The situation

Central Freight, a subsidiary of the Elco Group, is a large goods haulage company. It is organised on a regional basis, each region consisting of a number of operating depots which provide the services/products of the company. Regional and company head office staff act as a back up to the controllers of the depots.

Prior to 1974, the company offered only a general haulage service although it also operated a separate 'contracts' company. However, following a change in strategy it was decided to add 'new products', hopefully synergistically, stemming from a conversion of the main general haulage product. As a result each depot was then able to offer the following products:

1. *Contracts* – where an organisation's road haulage function is taken over by Central Freight.
2. *General haulage* – a national service, although now on a much smaller scale, previous haulage work having been converted to other products, especially contracts.
3. *Warehousing* – a storage facility for other companies, perhaps related to distribution or general haulage products.
4. *Property* – the rental of surplus storage space to a third party.
5. *Truck rental* – the hire of trucks of various sizes and types either on a self-drive or with-driver basis to individuals and organisations.

6. *Engineering* – the maintenance workshops for the company's fleet, surplus capacity being sold to the market place.

7. *Distribution* – the distribution of goods either held in Central Freight's or client companies' warehouses which could involve a 'breaking of bulk' service.

8. *Rescue* – roadside assistance to commercial vehicles on motorways and elsewhere, providing a repair service at the breakdown, or bringing a vehicle into the engineering depot for more serious repairs.

9. *Trailer rental* – the rental of trailers with or without truck rental.

10. *Miscellaneous,* covering any items of income or expenditure not covered under any other head.

A depot may have had any or all of these products, depending upon local demand. Thus in any one area, one product may predominate, whilst others may be insignificant or non-existent.

3.3 Case details

Part A: An investment centre approach

Each depot was treated by the company as an investment centre, as in turn were each of the products within each depot. Additionally, performance was compared with that budgeted for the investment centre as a whole and for its component parts.

Whilst depot managers had overall responsibility for all products within their depot, some products, depending on their nature or significance within the depot, also had individual product managers; thus the engineering product invariably had an engineering manager, due to the product's specialist nature, whilst other products were managed directly by the depot manager with some assistance from subordinates.

Transfer pricing

Each product and depot, as indicated above, was expected to sell its services to the market at a profit according to the local market conditions at any point in time. However, a considerable amount of inter-region, inter-depot and inter-product group (intra-depot) trading occurred. Whilst wishing to retain the profit motivation for such internal trading while encouraging (indeed, requiring) the use of such facilities (rather than that of outside suppliers), fixed internal charge rates were agreed centrally for some products, applicable nationwide. These rates were designed such that intra-depot trading had the lowest margins, with increasing margins for inter-depot and inter-region transactions, the latter still being lower than the current market price, or at least no lower than a favoured customer.

Sources of revenue

The above resulted in an investment centre's revenues being generated from four different sources in terms of price structure, i.e. sales to other products within the same depot, sales to other depots in the same region, sales to other regions, and sales to the general market. The proportions of these sales were largely dependent upon the particular location of a depot, the variety of products sold, and spare capacity available for sale to the outside market, etc.

Expenditures

Expenditures included the costs of inter-group and external subcontracting and the various operating expenses of each investment centre, including depreciation, and shared depot overheads (see Table 1). There were 'Group Directives' on a number of expenditure items over which profit centres had little or no control. These included rates of pay (and to an extent the hiring and firing of staff) and the source and/or price of a number of expenditures such as fuel, tyres and insurance. Company policies also existed regarding such factors as depreciation rates and the apportionment of depot, regional and head office overhead expenses across depots and product investment centres.

Capital equipment was authorised at regional and/or company level depending upon the size of expenditures proposed.

Operating statements

A periodic trading statement was produced for each depot, analysed between the ten product investment centres. This statement analysed revenue into eight categories of sale, i.e.

Revenues

(i) External Sales – to own customers
(ii) External Sales – to own customers, storage only
(iii) External Sales – transportation work subcontracted to another depot, e.g. backloads
(iv) External Sales – transportation subcontracted to outside contractors

= Total customer revenue

(v) Internal Sales – transportation work for other depots, e.g. backloads
(vi) Internal Sales – other revenues – intra-depot/products
(vii) Internal Sales – other revenues – inter-depot
(viii) Internal Sales – other revenues – inter-company

= Total revenues

The margin between operating expenditures and revenues was defined as the 'Gross Operating Profit'. Thereafter, apportioned charges were subtracted to provide a 'Trading Profit or Loss' which was then expressed as a percentage of (i) capital employed and (ii) revenues.

Capital employed consisted of (a) directly attributable fixed assets, i.e. those assets which could be specifically identified with a particular product investment centre, (b) fixed assets directly attributable to a depot (though apportioned to product investment centres) and (c) working capital and regional and company head offices fixed assets, apportioned over depots and thence product investment centres.

In outline, therefore, a depot operating statement appeared as in Table 1. This was compiled on a four-weekly basis showing a total for the depot as a whole and for each of the product investment centres.

Management appraisal

Management were assessed primarily on actual return on capital employed and profit percentage to revenue figures against budget, as well as certain physical/cost centre ratios.

Some regional managers produced a league table for senior management based upon the ROCE figures of the depots within their region. Although not published as such, depot managers were usually made aware of their relative position in the table: those at the bottom end of the table could expect more 'attention' and 'visitations' than other depots, whilst those at or near the top received relatively fewer.

Profit as percentage of revenue was considered to be of secondary importance to the ROCE ratio. Its trends were followed and considered to be an important indicator of the pricing practices adopted and of the present and future market situation. Low margins were in general considered with extreme concern.

Incentive schemes

A number of regions introduced incentive schemes based upon the achievement of budgeted profitability and other 'key target areas', particularly the level of debtors and certain cost ratios.

Table 1

Trading statement

Revenue:	Sales to outside customers
	Sales to outside customers – storage only
	External sales – transportation work subcontracted to another depot, e.g. backloads
	External sales – transportation subcontracted to outside contractors
	= Total customer revenue
	Internal sales – transportation work done for other depots, e.g. backloads
	Internal sales – other revenues – intra-depot/products
	Internal sales – other revenues – inter-depot
	Internal sales – other revenues – inter-company
	= Total revenues
Expenditure:	Subcontracting – own company
	Subcontracting – other contractors
	Total subcontracting
	Vehicle hire charges – medium to long term
	Vehicle hire charges – short term
	Drivers' wages
	Depot and warehouse wages
	Fuel and lubricants
	Tyres
	Other operating expenses
	Vehicle and equipment maintenance
	Depreciation
	Insurance and damages
	Licence duties
	Direct property charges
	Direct property depreciation
	Direct branch management and administration
	Direct branch miscellaneous
	Total operating expenses
Gross operating profit	Apportioned property charges
	Apportioned property depreciation
	Apportioned branch management and administration
	Apportioned branch miscellaneous
Net activity profit	Regional company/group head office expenses
Trading profit/loss	Trading profit as a percentage of revenue (%)
	Capital employed £
	Trading profit is a percentage of capital employed (£)

Part B: A profit centre approach

Profit centre changes

In 1983, following a reorganisation which included a contraction in the number of regions, changes were made to the product profit centre classifications:

1. 'Warehousing' and 'property' were merged into one profit centre.

2. 'Engineering' was segmented into two separate profit centres, internal and external sales, partly with a view to expansion in this product area and partly with a view to the potential acquisition of a specialist fleet maintenance organisation. To achieve the necessary separation of costs between external and internal sales, it was decided that materials (i.e. parts, etc.) and chargeable labour hours would be allocated to jobs and therefore profit centres, but that all other engineering operating costs, including non-productive labour hours, would be apportioned between the two functions.

3. 'Rescue' ceased to be considered as a profit centre in its own right, being placed under the 'engineering' profit centre in order not to create an additional product classification by the segmentation of engineering into two product profit centres

The managerial information rethink

Significant changes were made in the approach to performance measurement – effectively, the investment centre approach was replaced by a profit centre approach. In an interview (Section 3.4), the Finance Director set out his views of the objectives to be achieved by this change. This manifested itself particularly within the depot/product operating statements (see Tables 1 and 2) as follows:

(a) The apportionment of costs across product profit centres ceased, while remaining attributed to depots in total.

(b) 'Gross Operating Profit' replaced 'Trading Profit/Loss' as the bottom line for product profit centres. Gross Operating Profit represents the margin between revenues and all costs directly allocatable to a particular product profit centre. The exception, however, is in the two engineering product centres, where some costs allocatable to engineering as a whole were apportioned between the internal and external product profit centre. However, the direct allocation of labour hours and parts (materials) attribution is considered crucial to the performance measurement of engineering profit centres.

(c) A depot 'Trading Account', effectively a summary of the depot's operating statement, is now produced showing, for the period and cumulatively, actual vs. budget, the gross operating profits of each product profit centre and the depot as a whole. From this is deducted total 'Indirect Costs', effectively the previously apportioned costs, separated as regards 'property charges', 'management and administration', 'miscellaneous', and 'computer and Group head office' charges. From the remaining 'Depot Trading Profit', leasing interest charges and any extraordinary items are deducted to derive a 'Depot Net Profit' figure (Table 2).

(d) Statistics are also shown on the Trading Account for the actual period, and cumulative figures against the cumulative budget of each product expressed as a percentage of revenues. No attempt is now made to express profitability in relation to capital employed.

(e) For some years, Central Freight had adopted a policy of leasing rather than purchasing haulage vehicles. The mix of haulage vehicles (some owned, some leased) could have created anomalous measures, i.e. a depreciation cost and an increase in capital employed if the asset is owned, but a lease cost including interest but no capital employed if leased. To remove this anomaly, *for internal management accounting purposes only*, it had been the practice to treat leased assets as if they were owned assets, i.e. by the creation of 'dummy' asset and depreciation accounts. It was now agreed, however, that as relatively few owned haulage vehicles remained, such internal adjustments would cease. This effectively eliminated most of the capital employed directly attributable to haulage product profit centres, and a large proportion of depot capital employed.

(f) As part of the administrative reorganisation, all property, owned, leased or rented, was deemed to be that of a new profit centre, 'Group Property'. This function now made an internal charge to each profit centre for the space it occupied at what was considered to be a fair market rate on a 'current use value of the asset' basis. For occupiers of owned depots, this resulted in the removal of the site capital employed base and the inclusion of an annual rental charge in lieu. For those in leased or rented accommodation, a higher or lower rental charge would result, depending on the view of 'Group Property' as to what was a fair rental for the property. If managers could vacate a separable and relettable part of their premises, rental would be reduced accordingly.

Comparisons with budgeted performance continued.

Management objectives

Hitherto, objectives had been the maximisation of net profit to capital employed. Objectives are now stated as being the achievement of long-term growth (in business volume and profits) and improving/maintaining profitability (expressed as a percentage of profits to sales). It is made very clear, however, that such profitability is not to be achieved by looking for work at low margins, as it is believed that this would have long-term adverse repercussions on market prices. Indeed, minimum profitability requirements for contract hire have been established, this being anticipated as the company's major product growth area.

Table 2: Part 1

Period — *Depot Operating Summary* — *Depot:*

All values in £000		*Gross Operating Profit*			*% Return on Revenue*		
	Period Actual	*Period Budget*	*Cuml. Actual*	*Cuml. Budget*	*Period Actual*	*Cuml. Actual*	*Cuml. Budget*
Gross Operating Profit:							
Contracts	x	x	x	x	x	x	x
General Haulage	x	x	x	x	x	x	x
Warehouse & Property	x	x	x	x	x	x	x
Truck Rental	x	x	x	x	x	x	x
Distribution	x	x	x	x	x	x	x
Engineering: Int	x	x	x	x	x	x	x
Ext	x	x	x	x	x	x	x
Trailer Rental	x	x	x	x	x	x	x
Miscellaneous	x	x	x	x	x	x	x
= Total Gross Operating Profit	x	x	x	x	x	x	x
Indirect cost:							
Property	x	x	x	x			
Management & Admin.		x	x	x			
Computer and Group HO	x	x	x	x			
Depot Trading Profit	x	x	x	x			
Internal Charges:	x	x	x	x	x	x	x
Leasing		x	x	x			
Loan	x	x	x	x			
Current		x	x	x			
Other	x	x	x	x			
Extraordinary Items	x	x	x	x			
Depot Net Profits	x	x	x	x	x	x	x

Table 2: Part 2

Depot Profit Centre Operating Statement (All analysed by profit centre)

Revenue:	Sales to outside customers
	Sales to outside customers – storage only
	External sales – transportation work subcontracted to another depot, e.g. backloads
	External sales – ditto, but subcontracted to outside contractors
	= Total customer revenue
	Internal sales – transportation work for other depots, e.g. backloads
	Internal sales – other revenues – intra-depot/products
	Internal sales – other revenues – inter-depot
	Internal sales – other revenues – inter-company
	= Total revenues
Expenditure:	Subcontracting – own company
	Subcontracting – other contractors
	Total subcontracting
	Vehicle hire charges – medium to long term
	Vehicle hire charges – short term
	Drivers' wages
	Depot and warehouse wages
	Fuel and lubricants
	Tyres
	Other operating expenses
	Engineering costs: materials
	CF workshops
	outside
	Vehicle and equipment maintenance
	Maintenance equalisation
	Group equipment rental charges
	Insurance and damages
	Licence duties
	Direct property charges and depreciation
	Direct branch management and administration
	Direct branch miscellaneous
	Bad debts
	= Total operating expenses
Gross operating profits	

3.4 *An excerpt from an interview with the Financial Director*

Q What is the policy of Central Freight regarding inter-company trading?

A There is a price discounting arrangement for some inter-company transactions which matches the discounts given to external customers, so in that respect there are normal trading relationships between depots.

Q Is it company policy to use inter-company facilities when these are available in priority to others?

A There is no specific requirement for them to do so because each branch is a profit centre in its own right and can organise its business as it sees fit.

Q I understand there is one fixed rate per hour for inter-company engineering work although most regions adopt lower rates for intra-depot and intra-region work, all of which are below normal market charge-out rates.

A Yes. It is important to have a rate which gives the profit centre a contribution but places the emphasis on a least cost service of the wheel products. In other words, the wheel products (particularly hire) are the main products, and it is necessary to have consistency in the costings which are going into the product to ensure that it doesn't become uncompetitive. Hence, as maintenance is a major cost of these products, it was felt essential to have a uniform rate, and one which was not in any way excessive.

Q Are regions allowed to charge lower engineering rates than that fixed for the company as a whole?

A In theory, no. It is a measure of the company's approach to control that some regions feel free to lower the rates to reflect market conditions. However, this is an aspect we are currently debating. At the moment engineering revenue is split 60 per cent internal, 40 per cent external. But as we are expanding this area the balance is changing. We anticipate a one-third internal revenue, two-thirds external revenue, situation to arise.

Q Will the expansion of engineering services and the reduction of the percentage of inter-company work affect either the physical organisation of the product or the managerial control and measurement of it?

A We are considering whether or not we should physically separate the internal and external sales products. In certain locations this would be difficult; we are not going to put a fence down the middle of a workshop, but we could identify workshops which have predominantly external sales and manage them in a different way. Those with mostly internal sales could be treated as a cost centre of their depot, for example. This would diffuse the suspicion that, on hire and wheel products in particular, there is a dual profit which is making the final product less profitable. At depot level it doesn't matter very much, but at regional offices, product managers may feel their product is being made less profitable for the 'benefit' of others.

Q A significant area of inter-company trading is now property occupancy and vehicle 'ownership' costs. How are these charges set, and is this a basis for contention too?

A All property is notionally owned by Group Property, and vehicles financed by Group Leasing. Property charges are probably contentious. Depots have no control over these charges, which are set by quantity surveyors within group property. It is a recognised weakness in our system. Vehicle leasing is for tax purposes passed through our leasing company, but charges to depots are those actually received from the particular financing arrangement.

Q On the operating statement 'warehousing' and 'property' have been merged. Is this because of the Group Property charge?

A No. There is some cloudiness around the edges of warehousing and property anyway. If we have a warehouse we can either use it or, if it is a discrete building, hand it back to Group Property. If we retain it, whether it is for 'warehousing' or 'property' is immaterial. Whichever it is, it is using that space.

Q *In contrast, you now separate the engineering profit centre into internal and external. What were the reasons for this? When so many cost apportionments are required to enable each to be treated as a profit centre, this separation seems incongruous when other apportionments have now been removed from current operating statements.*

A This harks back to what I was saying earlier, i.e. the plans to expand this product area through acquisition and development. However, as only revenues, materials and maybe some labour can be allotted to 'internal' and 'external' with any confidence, the profitability measures are generally recognised as being unsatisfactory. We are thinking of merging them again, and then reconsidering them, if and when we categorise engineering profit centres as being either internal cost centres or external profit centres, depending on their revenue base as I outlined earlier. If we did this, of course, we would still expect engineering cost centres to utilise spare capacity by taking on profitable external work.

Q *But what would be their incentive to do so?*

A To reduce the overall cost of the engineering function.

Q *But that would mean that engineering profitability would subsidise a depot's wheel products?*

A That's right. Subsidisation would require stronger control procedures than currently. This is only a line of thought at the moment. We are still in the early stages of planning.

Q *Do you see this as an urgent problem?*

A It is the key problem at the moment.

Q *The other major change in managerial control has been in the change from an investment centre approach to a profit centre approach, but without apportionments of overheads over products. What were the reasons for this, please?*

A The investment centre approach was effectively obsolete as we owned so few assets (as we were leasing vehicles and using subcontractors) and had so little attributable capital employed. In any event, some property went back to 1890 so its historical cost was not a good basis for an investment centre approach. The view was taken that the concentration should be on contribution of products rather than its overall profitability. Because we have multi-product branches it is difficult to say how each product would stand up in its own right. Most branches have a core product but it is not necessarily the same product for each depot. The decision-making process as far as the products are concerned has to be based on the revenue and costs which are directly attributable to that product. It is all very well to 'know' that if you apportion overheads to a product it makes a loss, but if you take that product away, you don't necessarily save those indirect costs.

Q *But what caused the change when apportionment/absorption of overheads by products had been used for so long?*

A Probably growing dissatisfaction with it. General haulage was continually showing a loss, but if we did remove the product we wouldn't have saved many depot overheads. So it doesn't help you make decisions. However, it would be valid to say that if a depot had general haulage and no other products, it is unlikely to be profitable.

Q *Each product and depot was measured by its net profitability to capital employed. As this measure is no longer available and with the change to a profit centre basis, you appear to be evaluating performance on a basis of product contribution/depot contribution and profit as a percentage of sales. Is this an adequate measure for performance appraisal?*

A The expectation is that a depot will grow its business year on year by increasing the volume of business in the depot and thereby increase the profit generated by that depot.

Q So you are not just looking for profit percentage on sales achievement. You are looking at that related to the volume of business as well?

A The prime requirement is that the branch grows year on year. As our main growth product is contract hire with no balance sheet/capital requirement limitations or implications, growth while improving profit margins to desired levels is the main objective. If a depot says it cannot grow, that is a trigger point for a managerial review of the situation.

Q If growth is the main objective, what is to stop depots growing by attracting business at low prices with low profit margins?

A There are tight controls on hire products requiring minimum profit margins.

Q But as increased business does not require more Central Freight capital, why should you not seek marginal business?

A That is a debate we are currently going through. But, if we did so, we could pull the whole market price down.

Q You mentioned that leasing has no balance sheet implications. Is this true?

A Because of the arrangement we have and the Articles of Association of the leasing company, it is not controlled by Central Freight as far as the Companies Acts are concerned. Thus leased assets are not treated as fixed assets of the business.

Q But there are working capital implications?

A Yes. Indeed, one region charges its depots interest on the basis of attributable working capital outstanding.

Q Finally, is management at all levels measured solely by profitability, or are, as used to be the case, working capital control and physical/cost operating statistics also considered important? Also, are management renumerated according to their achievement of objectives?

A It depends upon the level of management. Key objectives are agreed with all managers. Although practices differ between regions, a number of objectives may be set for any one year which may be linked to their renumeration package. However, profitability growth year on year remains the overriding objective of regional, depot and product managers.

3.5 Questions

Part A

1. What are the pros and cons of comparing relative performance via a league table of ROCE?
2. What are the likely objectives and effects of Group management imposing national rates for the servicing of vehicles?
3. If management wish to measure performance on an investment centre basis, what changes would you recommend be made?
4. On what criteria should the performance measures and incentive reward systems of managers of branches and products within branches be based? Suggest suitable measures for branch managers and the managers of each product.

Part B

5. Why did the management of Central Freight consider it necessary to abandon ROCE as a basis for performance measurement?

6. Assess the merits of Profit to Sales as a basis for performance measurement. How might the negative aspects of this measure be mitigated by Central Freight? What other bases for performance measurement could you suggest as alternatives to that adopted by the company? What might you have done in their situation?

7. Suggest ways by which the performance of the engineering (vehicle repair) function and its management could be measured and the practical difficulties of doing so.

8. Is it logical or fair to measure the performance of branch and product managers as profit centres?

4
Belcom

4.1 Synopsis

This case study relates a particular approach to the calculation of standard total product costs and its impact upon product transfer prices and profits of a UK operating unit within a large group of companies.

Fundamental to the standard product costing system is Belcom's definition of direct and indirect costs, the selection of a base for the absorption of overhead, the use of cost behaviour information and the impact of intra-group rivalry. Transfer prices, based upon standard product costs as required by Group policy on inter-company transactions, have a fundamental impact on the performance of a profit centre with 60 per cent of its output being sold to inter-group companies.

4.2 Background

The situation

Belcom is an operating unit within the Electrocare Division of the Comeco Group of companies, operating from a UK base in Britain and overseas. Situated in the Home Counties and employing over 200, Belcom manufactures high-precision electronic components for sale to a broad range of industries, although its principal customers are in telecommunications and aerospace. The Belcom operating unit was established some four years ago in the UK by its sister company Scancom, Electrocare's Scandinavian operating unit, in the expectation that labour and overhead costs would be lower than in Scandinavia. Belcom operates on a much smaller scale of operations, its sales volumes being approximately one-fifth that of Scancom's. Belcom's position within the Division and Group, and *vis-à-vis* Scancom, may be inferred from the recent setting-up by Belcom of its own product research and development department. Hitherto, this function had been undertaken only by Scancom, which had effectively dictated what Belcom's product range would be.

Belcom is treated as a separate budget/profit centre by Comeco, but it is not itself a registered limited company. It does not have complete cash flow control (this is organised centrally by Comeco), although it does control its own income and revenue expenditures. Profitability is measured on a ROCE basis; there are no charges from Division or Group and no cost of capital charges. Of its 1983/4 sales turnover of £8m, over 60 per cent (£5m) was to inter-group companies, £2.4m of which was to Scancom . Reciprocally, a total of £1.7m of finished products for sale were bought from Scancom during 1983/4 to complement Belcom's product range. The Group reporting system for financial and monthly management accounts has no influence upon the detailed cost and management accounting systems of its operating units, other than to require conformity of expense categories.

4.3 *Case details*

The products

Belcom manufacture high-precision electronic components. These products require a high level of precision in their manufacture on which their quality and acceptability depends. For this reason there is a high level of quality control, resulting in frequent stoppages and test runs if components are not up to quality standards. Their manufacturing operation consists primarily of moulding and assembly operations. The moulding and assembly departments are treated as separate cost centres within Belcom, each with their own operational management.

The operations within each department are considered to be fairly homogeneous, there being no machinery or labour solely devoted to one product or product group as against another, e.g. all products are assembled on the same production line.

The differences between the two departments are, however, very marked. The moulding shop is relatively capital intensive, employing only 13 machine operators, while the assembly department has relatively little equipment but employs over 70 direct workers.

The proportions of resource inputs into the wide variety of products made can be very different as between assembly and moulding department operations. As will be discussed shortly, while standards exist for assembly department labour inputs, similar figures for the moulding department do not exist.

Policy on inter-company transactions

The company's 'Policy on Inter-Company Trading' is stated in a policy document (see Section 4.4) which is '. . . a broad statement of policy, and individual units have the freedom to negotiate specific inter-company trading systems to meet their most important business needs within the overall policy'.

Under this policy, inter-company pricing should be on a standard factory cost plus basis, the 'plus' being 15 per cent (in contrast with the 'normally anticipated' 30 per cent on sales to non-group customers) in addition to related distribution costs. There are no inter-company negotiations as such on prices, but because some items are made in both Belcom and Scancom and transferred between each, a 'raising of eyebrows' at the transfer price actually used has promoted intense discussion about the factory standard costs, resulting in comparisons of cost elements and physical input details behind the standards.

The costing approach

The entire costing system is one which Scancom initiated when it first set up Belcom as the UK operating unit. As such it is believed by Belcom's management to be identical in most respects to that in Scancom, although some differences may occur in the treatment of specific costs as being direct or indirect, variable or fixed. In all significant aspects, however, the Belcom and Scancom costing systems are believed to be the same.

The costing approach is basically factory product standard absorption costing, related to which the treatment of the moulding department costs and the identification of the fixity and variability of cost elements are critical.

An understanding of the standard costing system is necessary to appreciate the cost information used within the company.

The standard costing system

The standard costing system adopts a total/absorption overhead approach at a factory cost level. The system naturally reflects the decision as to which costs are considered direct as against indirect.

Direct costs are deemed to be:

(a) Direct Materials, including an allowance for a 'normal' scrap rate, and
(b) Direct Labour for the assembly department only, but including in the rate per hour, shift premiums, employers' employment costs (National Insurance and Pensions) and holiday payments.

The exclusion of the thirteen moulding department machine operators from the 'direct' category is in line with the system adopted in Scancom. There were two reasons for this approach:

1. There is a distinct problem of relating moulding direct labour to individual parts; the production of precision items is accompanied by intense quality control, test runs, considerable differences in batch sizes and frequent stoppages for a wide variety of reasons. It is believed that there can be no consistency of unit labour input times (and costs) under these circumstances and therefore no 'standards' are possible.
2. It was felt that there would be a need from time to time to compare costs between the two units, and that for this reason they should be built up on the same basis.

The standard times of the assembly department are those set in the UK and are not related to or influenced by the Scancom standards. Indeed, Belcom are unaware of the 'standards' in Scancom although Belcom are regularly accused of having 'slacker' standards than their sister company. Specific comparisons are rarely made, although in global terms, Scancom's high profitability is used to infer that Belcom has lower levels of efficiency and more lax product material and labour usage and price standards.

However, such comparison may not be valid since the selection of products for Belcom to produce is not identical to that of Scancom, and in fact results from the latter's decisions as to which products shall be made where.

The assembly direct labour standards are the basis for the absorption of indirect costs on a blanket rate basis, i.e. as all moulding costs are treated as an indirect cost, there is, effectively, only one 'productive direct labour' department.

Cost behaviour information

The variability and fixity of costs is an important aspect of the company's standard cost and budgetary information. Its application, however, does not result from any managerial belief in the importance of such information from an operational decision-making viewpoint: it derives solely from their recognition that current and budgeted operations are substantially below full normal operating capacity. To achieve product cost figures comparable with their competitors who they believe are operating at or near full capacity, it was decided to budget for a fixed cost volume variance (under recovery) and to absorb into product costs (a) variable overheads, and (b) only the proportion of fixed costs which reflect the capacity utilisation assumed in the budget.

All factory indirect costs are identified for this purpose as being either fixed or variable. However, there is no formal approach to the identification of the behaviour of costs. 'I ask myself the question,' said the Financial Director, 'do I believe that an expenditure item is varying with time or volume. It's as simple as that.'

The Budgeted Assembly Department Indirect Costs Statement, Schedule E, indicates which assembly indirect costs are considered to be a fixed cost. Depreciation and salaries are considered fixed. Assembly direct labour costs are considered to be variable in spite of the labour being paid a basic wage on a time basis with no payment by result element. All moulding shop operative costs are considered to be variable, as indeed are non-management quality control and production services labour costs. The not insignificant cost of moulding department repair and maintenance, consumable materials and some hire of assets are also treated as being variable.

The budgetary process

The budgetary system is a fairly traditional 'meeting ground' approach. The demand for Belcom's products is estimated for the budget period, and checked against production capacity to confirm that demand can be met. This is then crystallised into a production plan and costed as to materials, labour and overheads. There are no group or divisional pressures to 'fudge' budgets, just to achieve a good profit-earning budget – this despite operations running at only 55 per cent of full capacity.

The factory capacity is calculated (Schedule A) on the basis of what is considered to be 'a desirable mode of working'. This is assumed to be, for this purpose, two shifts, day and evening, making use of currently available space and physical resources. 'Reasonable' norms for absenteeism and efficiency are set. A further adjustment is made to convert what is otherwise considered to be 'ideal' circumstances to a 'normal' level of operations. The budgeted standard hours, based on demand volumes, represents a 55 per cent utilisation of this capacity.

The implications of the 55 per cent capacity utilisation calculation in Schedule A may be seen in Schedule D, the Budgeted Factory Overhead Absorption Summary. The factory overheads are shown analysed between their fixed and variable cost elements. As 45 per cent of normal operating capacity is unutilised, this proportion of the £995,000 of fixed costs is considered to be a 'budgeted capacity utilisation variance' which should be a charge against Belcom as an operating unit and not against individual products.

This Scancom-inspired adjustment was instituted because it was felt that over the first five years of Belcom's existence, the learning curve effect and acceptance in the market would enable the capacity utilisation to be increased from an initial level of 40 per cent to the full normal operating capacity experienced by Scancom. On the basis of the Scandinavian experience, 85 per cent of ideal capacity was considered to be an attainable level of capacity utilisation (Schedule A); overhead rates and thence standard product costs were calculated which reflected this, on the assumption that such would provide cost data comparable and competitive with other suppliers in the market. Even at a 45 per cent under-utilisation however, the business was expected to be in a profit-making situation.

The budgeted direct labour cost calculations for 1984/5 are shown in Schedule B, which assumes a totally different working hours and shift arrangement and numbers of direct employees to that in Schedule A. From this is derived a standard direct labour rate per hour, inclusive of holiday and employer costs of £4.69 per hour, based upon a demand for 85,830 standard hours. A direct labour staffing level of 71 for 1984/5 is budgeted, out of a total staff complement of 210.8 on average for 1984/5 (see Schedule C).

The impact on the absorption rate of this capacity approach can be seen from an examination of Schedule D. Of the £1,617,000 of overhead, £448,000 representing 45 per cent of the fixed overhead element is deducted, leaving overheads to be absorbed of £1,169,000. On the basis of 85,830 standard labour hours and a total labour cost of £402,840 which gives a standard labour hour rate of £4.69 (see Schedule B), a budgeted overhead absorption rate of 290 per cent on direct labour cost may be derived.

Quality costs

The high precision demanded of the products has a significant impact upon the levels of waste and scrap experienced. Most of this reflects moulding problems, and occurs during or at the completion of the moulding operation, even though it may not be identified at that stage. A significant proportion only becomes apparent during or at the completion of the moulding operation, even though it may not be identified at that stage. A significant proportion only becomes apparent during subsequent assembly and final inspection operations. The scrap identified at the moulding stage is 'valued' for scrap cost calculation purposes at the direct cost of material only (it having attracted no direct labour (as defined) up to this point), whilst that identified later is valued at material, labour to date plus an overhead recovery.

The product standards for each year reflect anticipated scrap levels, usually based upon previous years' experiences. However, while all scrap should be recorded on scrap notes, it is believed that very significant amounts of scrap are not recorded, evidenced by a 'stock deficiency', i.e. a difference between the physical and book figures, at year-end stock take, of £600,000. Management believes that the lack of recording stems from the time demands on the moulding department to 'meet the product standards and output demands'. Although Belcom's management are very concerned about this aspect, the scrap recording system is known to have loopholes and is frequently by-passed; as moulding operatives are treated as weekly paid staff, there is no requirement for payment purposes to identify work done related to scrapped output.

Management's view

In principle, Belcom's management have the authority to alter the absorption costing system should they think fit, although resistance is likely from Scancom should transfer prices increase as a result. However, it is only a few top management personnel who really see the anomalies of the costing method; they dislike it and would like to change it. There are those of the top management team who see it as 'merely costing' and not really having much influence on company performance. The Managing Director, for example, adopts a stance of 'no matter what the costs say, price is what we can get and it is really not influenced by cost figures, which are always capable of manipulation'.

The whole aspect of capacity reduction is currently being examined, because the actual utilisation during 1984/5 is less than 55 per cent and the market on the horizon does not look good. First indications are that real capacity reduction will be difficult, even impossible, in terms of space and machinery, plant and equipment, but that labour level reductions will soon have to start being implemented. Again, the latter will be difficult in terms of indirect and management labour because of the technical and quality aspects.

Schedule A: Budget 1984/5

Factory capacity and utilisation based on the assembly department direct labour

Direct heads per shift	60
Shifts (days and evenings)	2

Available hours	*Days*	*Evenings*	*Total*
Hours per day	7	6.75	
Number of working days	230	230	
Absenteeism	5%	5%	
Efficiency	100%	100%	
Normal operating ideal*	85%	85%	
Total capacity hours	78,000	75,240	153,240
Budgeted standard hours (based on demand volumes)			85,830
Utilisation of capacity			55%

*This adjustment reduces what is considered to be 'ideal' capacity level to one which in most circumstances would be considered a maximum practical operating level of operations.

Schedule B

Budget 1984/5
Direct labour cost

	Days	Directs Evening	Twilight
No. of directs	49	77	77
Hours per week	37.5	36.25	26.2
Total hours/week	1,837.5	399	288.2
No. of weeks/quarter	13	13	13
Hours/quarter	23,888	5,184	3,747
× rate of pay = £2.96			
Oct – Dec 84	70,707	15,344	11,090
Shift allowance 20%		3,069	
			£100,210
2nd, 3rd and 4th quarter			
× rate of pay £3.14	75,008	16,278	11,766
Shift allowance 20%		3,256	
			£106,308
Total pay per last three quarters = 106,308 ×× 3 =			318,924
+ 1st quarter			100,210
			419,134
+ 16.5% NI & pensions			69,157
			488,219
Less absenteeism/Non-payment Factors			85,451
			£402,840

Total pay	£402,840
divided by standard hours	85,830
Rate per standard hour	£4.69

Schedule C

Budget 1984/5
Personnel

	Actual Mar 1984	*3rd R/F Sept 1984*	*Budget Sept 1985*	*Budget Ave 1985*
Factory direct	75	74	71*	71
Factory indirect	50	57	58	57
Quality control	20	20	21	21
Factory total	145	151	150	149
Technical management	2	2	2	2
R & D	2	4	7	6.3
Total technical dept	4	6	9	8.3
Marketing	8	7	9	9
Home sales	13	14	15	15
Export sales	3	3	4	3.5
Warehouse & distribution	7	7	7	7
Total sales & marketing	31	31	35	34.5
General manager	2	2	2	2
Finance	7	7	8	8
Systems	1	2	2	2
Personnel	7	7	7	7
Total administration	17	18	19	19
Total	197	206	213	210.8

*Decrease planned without redundancy through use of fixed-term temporary contracts.

Schedule D

1984/85 Budget
Factory Overhead Absorption

Cost centre	*Variable*	*Fixed*	*Total*
	£k	*£k*	*£k*
Quality control	203	16	219
Quality development & engineering	–	45	45
Toolroom	4	63	67
Production services	176	333	509
Production engineering	–	47	47
Moulding	184	103	287
Assembly	55	249	304
Production planning	–	92	92
Production management	–	47	47
	622	995	1,617
Under utilisation			
(based on 45% of fixed costs)		448	
Total factory overheads			1,617
Less under-absorbed fixed costs			(448)
			£1,169
Total direct labour (absorbed)			
Standard hours produced	85,830		
Standard rate per hour	£4.69		
Total direct labour		£403	

Overhead absorption rate $\frac{\pounds 1{,}169\text{k}}{\pounds 403\text{k}}$ = 290% of direct labour cost

Schedule E

Budget 1984/85
Indirect Expenditure – Assembly Dept

		£
Small tools	F	400
Consumable materials		18,800
Bin liners		3,900
Solvents		3,000
Alcohol		11,500
Spare strips		6,000
Salaries	F	97,185
Overtime premium	F	4,500
Pension costs	F	9,525
N.I. costs	F	8,745
Recruitment	F	1,200
Training course fees	F	3,000
Welfare clothing		500
Welfare medical		600
Travel		4,000
Entertaining – internal		800
Entertaining – exports		100
Purchased repairs		2,000
Maintenance contracts		2,250
Depreciation (historic)	F	120,600
Telephone	F	600
Stationery	F	400
P & L on asset disposal	F	3,000
		£302,605
	Fixed	249,155
	Variable	53,450

4.4 Appendix

Policy on inter-company transactions

Introduction

As the volume of inter-company business within the Comeco Group develops it is important to establish some basic ground rules on inter-company trading. It is not intended that this document should be anything other than a broad statement of policy, and individual units have the freedom to negotiate specific inter-company trading systems to meet their most important business needs within this overall policy.

Primary long-term aims of the policy

It is intended that all operating units should achieve a high degree of mutual trust based on a clear understanding of the company's marketing needs and production capabilities. In line with the company's organisation policy, it is intended that all production units, i.e. centres of excellence, should be available, as a source of product supply, to all marketing units, without parochial or regional preferences.

Major policy objectives

- To ensure that each operating unit understands and employs the inter-company pricing policy.
- To ensure that each manufacturing unit revises and maintains standard costs in the same way, and in line with policy.
- To ensure that each marketing unit schedules and orders products from manufacturing units in a fair and reasonable way, and in line with the policy.
- To ensure that an equitable view is taken on inter-company rejects and returns.

Specific policies

(1) *Inter-company pricing*

All inter-company pricing should be on a cost-plus basis, as already agreed, and changes to the inter-company pricing formula should not be made without the approval of the Managing Director.

Manufacturing units must give marketing units at least three months' notice, in writing, of any changes in inter-company prices.

(2) *Revision of standard costs*

Clearly, if inter-company transactions are carried out on a cost-plus basis, it is important that standard costs are maintained by the manufacturing units on the same basis.

It is understood that, at the moment, standard costs are not prepared by manufacturing units in exactly the same way, but it is the intention to work towards a common format. The normal interval between each general revision of standard costs should normally be one year, i.e. the budget cycle, and only where changes are of exceptional significance or importance should a general revision be undertaken in a period of less than one year. During the life of the standard cost it is intended that variances, whether they be favourable or adverse, should be absorbed by the manufacturing unit.

Standards should be revised when:

(a) Manufacturing methods are *significantly* changed due to plant layout, machinery alterations, change in product design, use of different materials, etc.
(b) The relationship of normal capacity and actual activity is *significantly* out of balance.
(c) The disparity between the standard and expected performance is so *significant* that the standard as a measurement loses its value.
(d) An existing standard is discovered to be incorrectly set and a *significant* difference exists.

Revisions should be *held to a minimum*, despite the fact that standards may not be precise, in order to provide for relative comparisons between operating periods and/or versus budget.

The frequency of general or individual revisions to standard costs is dependent upon:

(a) The significance and permanency of change in cost levels of direct labour, direct material and factory indirects/overheads.
(b) The significance and number of changes in standards.
(c) The significance of change in factory overhead structure due to changes in capacity.
(d) The time, cost and effort involved in revising standards where the quantity of parts, sub-assemblies and goods affected is of significance.

All marketing units have the right to request and be given from the manufacturing units the standard costs of the products that they purchase.

4.5 *Questions*

1. As a consultant to the company, with a wide-ranging brief, what changes would you recommend to Belcom's management with a view to increased profitability? What are likely to be the impact and problems of implementing the changes you recommend?

2. You are the 'Management Auditor' of Comeco, responsible to the Group Managing Director. Following cryptic comments from the newly appointed auditors, the MD has charged you with the responsibility of reporting upon the profitability performance of Belcom, making such recommendations for change as you think fit. Prepare such a report.

3. In what respects, and for what reasons, might you expect the recommendations for change proposed by the consultant appointed by Belcom (See Q1), and those of the Management Auditor (See Q2), to be different?

4. What alternative transfer pricing methods are available to a large international group of companies? How appropriate is the cost-plus approach adopted by Comeco? How, if at all, would you suggest that the current policy be changed? Should such a Group allow parts of their organisation to adopt different transfer pricing practices?

5. What is implied by the term 'capacity' in a manufacturing business? How relevant is the definition adopted by Belcom and what are the implications for the company's planning and decision-making?

6. How appropriate is the company's approach to product costing in relation to pricing decisions and product profitability measurement?

7. What approaches are potentially available to management in determining the fixity and variability of the costs of their organisation? How appropriate do you consider the approach adopted by Belcom?

8. How appropriate is the treatment of the Moulding Department costs by Belcom? In what respects might their approach be different? Consider the implications and difficulties of implementing any changes you have suggested.

9. What are the implications of the case study in relation to the performance measurement of Belcom and its management by Comeco's management?

10. Examine the view of some of Belcom's senior management that costing does 'not really have much influence on company performance'.

11. What would be the likely problems of recording scrap in an environment such as that described for Belcom?

5
The Kimco Group

5.1 *Synopsis*

A significant factor in the success of large diversified groups is the system of management control used. Adopting and operating the controls has a number of problems. A contingency approach to management accounting might suggest that the environment and overall policies of a business organisation will have a major impact on the selection of control mechanisms. The case of Kimco describes methods of control employed in a conglomerate group whose normal business activity includes acquisition and disposition of subsidiaries.

Management accounting approaches to divisional control are described. Given that mechanisms for determining transfer prices can play a significant part in co-ordinating group activities, it may be considered surprising that little group effort is put in this direction. The company is able to reconcile this with their general strategy through the function which the internal audit unit performs.

The questions on this case pay attention to the group's policy on decentralisation and the relationship of this policy to the divisional accounting control and internal audit activities.

5.2 *Background*

The company

The Kimco Group has placed considerable importance on decentralisation, enabling operating unit managers to contribute to the Group's success by allowing them a large degree of autonomy in their activities. The significance of their control mechanisms can be considered in relation to their compatibility with these objectives.

Kimco is a large international conglomerate with a total turnover in excess of £2 billion organised into ten Operating Groups, each of which consists of a number of Operating Companies. These businesses range from mature established products/industries to those in fast-growing new technology areas, and from capital-intensive to labour-intensive operations. Each Operating Company is treated as far as possible as an autonomous budget/investment centre. With this organisational structure, there is a head office staff of less than 50.

Each Operating Group is represented on the main Board of Directors by its Chairman, although they are expected to, and do, take an overall, non-parochial view of the Board's planning and decision-making.

Although the Board and Operating Group managers receive periodic control data, their managerial control is primarily effected through the formal planning process. The operation of this approach is described in the case. A key feature is that allocations of resources and setting of performance targets are determined at the planning stage as a result of detailed enquiry. Subsequent management is by exceptions, which are expected to be rare.

Each Operating Company has a team of specialists (accounting, marketing, operating, research) which reports directly to its Operating Company Managing Director. Likewise, at Operating Group level, there is a management team containing accounting and marketing specialists led by the Operating Group Managing Director, who chairs the Operating Group Board which includes all the Operating Company Managing Directors. Each member of the management team reports to the Operating Group Managing Director and Chairman. However, only accountants have a dual responsibility, to the Managing Director of the Operating Company, as well as to Group HQ as members of the accounting function. Thus, as part of this, an Operating Company's accountant will act functionally, in as much as he is expected to:

(a) produce routine accounts and reports in prescribed format/timetables, *and*
(b) report on any actions which are either in contradiction to such 'rules' or 'requirements' as are laid down in group accounting and procedural practices which the accountant believes are financially ill advised and against the company's interests.

Objectives

Each Operating Group and, in turn, their Operating Companies have as their prime objective the maximisation of profitability expressed in terms of a return on their net operating assets, effectively ROCE, subject to one major constraint, that of cash flow/financial funding. The principal profitability measure relates profits before taxation to capital employed, on both historic accounting and inflation-adjusted bases. However, the Main Board also receives routine reports for each Operating Company showing profit performance after deducting amounts imputed for tax and dividends (again, these are expressed in historic and inflation-adjusted terms).

5.3 Case details

The annual planning process is, to a very large extent, a bottom-up approach, in that the plans prepared at each lower level are subject to the approval of the next higher level within the Group. In particular, the plans of Operating Companies are subject to approval at the Operating Group level, whilst the plans of the Operating Groups are subject to the approval of the Main Board.

These plans contribute to the formation of a five-year long-term plan in broad outline, the first year of which, in substantially more detail, is the annual budget/action plan.

Whilst the assumptions on which the plans are based, and the basic strategic and tactical aspects contained therein including market share and cash flow, are subject to substantial scrutiny and critical appraisal by the Main Board, the ability of the Operating Group to achieve the planned level of long-term profitability is the principal factor under consideration. Cash flow, however, is the dominant constraint. In turn, the Operating Board applies the considerations given by the Main Board to the plans of the Operating Companies within its sphere.

Cash flow constraints

A prime feature of the company's planning is that it is generally anticipated that the plans, both short and long term, shall be achievable within existing capital and cash flow resources.

Thus, Operating Companies can plan on the assumption that, should they wish, they are able to reinvest their positive cash flows in their business, subject to approval being gained for their plans through the process mentioned above. For this purpose, positive cash flows are deemed to be net of the imputed taxation and dividend payments. Within these cash limits, improved performance can arise through increased profitability or enhanced productivity.

Capital budgeting

The planning of capital expenditures is an integral and explicit part of the planning process. Proposed capital investments receive approval when agreed as part of an Operating Company's plan. The criteria for acceptance is not a specific payback, rate of return, DCF yield or NPV. Funds are made available only if the investment is deemed to be part of, and necessary to, the achievement of an acceptable corporate plan, itself primarily measured on a ROCE basis.

Capital expenditures contained within the plan, having received such tacit approval, may be implemented by Operating Companies without the need for referral to any higher authority. The issue then becomes, 'Does the Operating Company still want and need to make this capital expenditure, and is it achievable within the limits of their internally generated cash flow?'

The need for capital expenditures are expected to be anticipated at the planning stage and should therefore receive tacit approval by being part of an approved plan. Exceptions should be rare and for minor items, and as such may be authorised at Operating Company level, providing that funding can be achieved without failing to meet agreed cash flow plans.

Where a plan requires resources over and above the net cash flow generated by an Operating Company or Operating Group, a more formal and orthodox approval system is usually applied. Firstly, the expenditure would need to gain formal approval as part of the strategic/tactical plan of the company/group. This is usually treated as part of the planning cycle, but in exceptional cases as an *ad hoc* item. Secondly, a financial appraisal will be carried out including:

(a) the identification of the potential sources of funds to be used and their cost;
(b) the calculation of the NPV and DCF yield of the proposal; *and* possibly
(c) an assessment of the investments' risk profile.

Inter-company transactions and transfer pricing

Inter-Group transactions represent only 7½ per cent of group sales. However, the level of inter-company purchases and sales is very high indeed for some Operating Companies. These range from:

(a) those parts of the Group's business which are vertically integrated, i.e. where one Operating Company sells its output to another for further processing and/or sale to a final consumer;
(b) those Operating Companies which provide goods or services with applications/uses to a large number of other Operating Companies, e.g. transportation; *and*
(c) inter-group services including insurance, legal and taxation advice, management training and (some) computer facilities (although these tend to be of only minor significance within the company).

Company policies do not require Operating Companies to trade with each other, but grant them the freedom to look elsewhere for their customers/suppliers should they wish, although of course the company hopes that companies would find it *mutually* beneficial to trade with each other. The accent is on the term 'mutually beneficial': if one company does not wish to trade with another, for whatever reason, it need not do so. Each Operating Company is expected to 'stand on its own feet' in the market place.

Given this 'arm's length' approach to inter-company trading, transfer pricing policies within the conglomerate are not explicitly stated. Operating Companies trade with each other only if they wish. Group Management did not wish to directly intervene on price negotiation, so that in this respect Operating Companies had apparently the same freedom of action as if they were trading with an organisation outside of the group.

However, for those 'captive' suppliers or customers significantly dependent upon internal trade, there was a tendency to negotiate long-term arrangements on volumes and prices to avoid the sudden impact of loss of trade. Where either party is free to look elsewhere, 'mutually beneficial' is the keynote to the setting of inter-company agreements. Instances have arisen where one

Operating Company has not reached an agreed basis for trading with another, resulting in the failure and closure of one of the companies.

Autonomy and control

As stated earlier, each Operating Company is treated as far as possible as an autonomous budget/investment centre. In principal, as long as short- and long-term plans and achievements

(a) can be demonstrated to provide an acceptable return, *and*
(b) do not require additional funding,

an Operating Company is effectively free to adopt whatever policies or actions it considers necessary to pursue its objectives.

This does not mean, however, that Operating Group and Main Board management do not show a keen interest in their Operating Companies. Periodic results (on a 4, 4, 5 week cycle) are regularly monitored. A wide range of financial information is provided for the Main Board and Operating Group by their accountants, including a detailed historic and price level adjusted profit statement, balance sheet and a cash flow/sources and application of funds statement. From time to time further details or explanations are required from Operating Company management. Such 'explanations', however, are by way of informing senior management of, for example, changes in operating situations rather than to enable Operating Group or Board 'control' in an action/decision-making sense.

Company policy is for each profit centre manager to 'stand or fall' in relation to his unit's performance.

Many organisations may state that their profit centres are free to negotiate prices on an arm's length basis; however, in practice a number impose the constraint that inter-company trade shall take priority over external trade or that companies within a Group must be given the choice of trading at whatever price is quoted on the market (*Coates, Smith, Stacey*).[1] This significantly reduces the freedom and arm's length basis. Further, many companies provide a Group transfer pricing arbitration service, whose intervention may undermine the apparent independence conveyed by descriptions such as 'autonomous' and 'arm's length' negotiation.

Given the degree of autonomy granted to Kimco's Operating Companies, each Operating Unit can be considered to have many of the properties of a separate and individual investment within the company's portfolio. The management is evaluated on this basis by comparison with the achievements of other companies in that industry. Operating Company performance is viewed in terms of alternative uses of the capital invested. This provides data which is consistent with potential sell-off and shut-down decisions necessary for Group flexibility. Kimco wishes to be able to decide to divest itself of one of its Operating Companies, for strategic or profitability purposes, with some confidence that this should not affect the profitability of other parts of the company. Such a strategy may not be facilitated by a structure dependent upon inter-company transactions maintained by transfer pricing constraints.

In many respects, therefore, the Kimco conglomerate has placed itself in a very similar position to an institutional investor, in that it can add or subtract investments to and from its portfolio, treating each in its own right and without fear of implications elsewhere in its business. The principal difference is, of course, that institutional investors do not usually attempt to manage the companies in which they invest to the extent found in this company. Kimco, however, are prepared to be involved in their Operating Companies, if necessary, by exercising their prerogative of changing and improving their management.

The internal audit function

The autonomy granted in setting transfer prices could give the impression that Kimco exercises only relatively superficial and general control of its Operating Companies. Their inter-company transaction and transfer pricing policies open up the possibilities of pursuit of local objectives which are suboptimal from a Group standpoint. The reality is very different indeed. To understand this, an examination of the role of the internal audit function is essential since it may be seen as central to the managerial style adapted by the Group.

The internal audit 'department', part of the financial function, reporting directly to the Financial Controller effectively acts as:

(a) internal auditors;
(b) financial and general business advisers;
(c) managers of the training of accountants within the Group;
(d) advisers on promotions/managerial appointments.

These are not purely routine roles, as the following illustrates.

The *internal auditors* are not expected to duplicate the role of the external auditors or in any way prepare the ground for them. Although a certain amount of 'systems audit' work is involved, their main role, perhaps surprisingly, was described as being to 'identify risks and opportunities for management'. This includes locating opportunities for cost savings by dealing with, for example, other parts of the company (i.e. inter-company trading). Their approach is to identify the more important strategic and tactical decisions taken by management during a given period. These are then 'reviewed' in the light of the known circumstances both at the time of the decision and subsequently, with the purpose of 'flagging' to the Operating Company's management situations where, for example, opportunities or alternatives may have been overlooked or decisions taken on inadequate or erroneous data. While this represents principally a consultative and advisory role, on rare occasions, where it proves necessary, a 'more formal' report to an Operating Company will be made.

Financial and general business advice and assistance is freely available from the internal audit department. Any such advice is not specifically charged for, although it is included in the blanket/arbitrary apportionment of the department's costs to each Operating Company and Group. Advice may be sought on a wide variety of topics. Examples could vary from advice on good/group accounting practices to the collection of information for a new capital investment or strategic change, to assessing the risk of alternatives and their compatibility with group policies and to guidance as to the likely acceptability of budget proposals. Although to some extent 'advice' can be seen as a way of 'anticipating' the internal audit review, it is considered very much a means of disseminating the very wide experience contained within the internal audit department and as a means of obtaining additional inputs of time and expertise not available within a particular part of the company.

Internal audit has responsibility for the *training of accountants*, providing recruits with a wide range of general business, managerial and accounting experience. Each year a number of trainees who demonstrate an ability or interest in other directions can, and do, obtain posts in specialisms other than accounting or in general management, or switch to such after qualifying as accountants. While most of this training is received during secondment to one of the Operating Companies, time is spent at Operating Group and Company Head Offices and the audit department. Trainees are encouraged to apply for posts within the company as they arise. The internal audit manager will often make specific 'recommendations' to posts.

As *advisers on new appointments* both financial and management, the internal audit managers are in a unique position within the company. They will be aware of:

(a) the more mature trainees;
(b) ex-trainees in post throughout the group; *and*
(c) managers with whom they have contact in the course of their audit function.

They will have been able to form strong opinions on individuals' abilities, their strengths and weaknesses, their managerial, technical and inter-personal skills, their ambitions, potential and experience to date. There are therefore very strong reasons for the internal audit manager to be the first avenue consulted in the selection of appropriate candidates for posts when they arise, particularly in the accounting field: advertising costs are saved, recruitment time is reduced, candidates will have knowledge of the company's operations and reporting methods and, more importantly, are known to be suitable for the demands of a particular post. Further, from a company viewpoint, a high degree of 'accounting manpower planning' can be practised, particularly in ensuring that 'up and coming' accountants and managers receive appropriate career development and promotions. The likelihood that personnel with potential will 'look outside' the company for career progression is thus reduced and the company's investment in them retained. Additionally, personnel who have reached their managerial ceiling will not be promoted beyond their level of competence. Where suitable candidates are not available within the company, appropriate 'new blood' is recruited, but again, it is usual for the internal audit manager to be consulted both as to the method of selection and in the selection process itself. This has the added advantage that, because the manager has an overall knowledge and view of the company's longer-term needs and plans, a new employee can be selected who not only fills the gap of a particular post, but also fulfils a longer-term requirement within the company.

5.4 Concluding remarks

Control and the accounting mafia

Having considered the company's philosophy of managerial autonomy and examined the activities of the internal audit function, it is now possible to examine the manner in which the company maintains control.

The access to information available to the internal audit department managers of Kimco may give them the opportunity to be very influential members of the management team. Their own description of their function as 'The Accounting Mafia' is perhaps a reflection of their position within the company. This may be highlighted by considering the following:

(a) As internal auditors, they and their staff have access to all information held within the company, particularly that of a financial nature. Their role is to examine what has happened and what is intended to happen in order to criticise constructively; to suggest alternatives, and point out errors of omission or commission.
(b) As managers of trainees on placement, they have access to a regular feedback of profit centre activities via both the trainees' log books and their regular progress meetings.
(c) Ex-trainees in permanent posts throughout the company will be aware that their present post and their future promotional prospects are highly influenced by the internal audit manager. There is thus a vested interest in maintaining good relations by 'reporting openly' situations which they believe would or might be of concern or interest to the internal audit department. This in any event reinforces the training they received whilst working within the internal audit function.
(d) The functional line of reporting again emphasises their 'independence' from the decision of management teams which they advise. This allows them to take an independent position on a particular company.
(e) As advisers they are often highly involved in planning and decision-making and therefore also in the logistics of those plans, the decisions made and of the need to follow up their implementation.

It can be seen that there are many factors contributing to the creation of the framework for the particular type of control which Kimco has been operating. The value of the approach is evident from the Group's lively and successful performance record seen in terms of share price, profitability and turnover growth. The nature of their control does not readily fit with definitions which stress obtaining conformity to plans through action and evaluation. For Kimco the aim of control is to enable managers to exercise their entrepreneurial skills without undue constraints but consistent with the interests of the Group.

Operating management is not directly concerned with the raising of finance since this is provided through the Group, although it is necessary to accept cash flow constraints which permit the co-ordination of the planning of financial resources. It should be particularly noted that Kimco's scheme of control provides direction but minimises restriction, avoiding excessive interference with operating decisions. The system of arm's-length negotiation of transfer prices is consistent with this view of control. Other approaches, dependent to some extent on more centralised restriction, would undermine their managerial style. Moreover, it would corrupt the data and may inhibit changes relating to sell-off or shut-down decisions. Operating decisions themselves may be distorted by a more restrictive transfer pricing policy.

The transfer pricing policy is adopted not to attempt to achieve any 'synergistic' advantages that may be attributed to any individual decision from a Group point of view; rather, the policy enables the local managers to obtain input and output prices which are consistent with the Group's style as a conglomerate with a flexible investment approach. Further, operating managers are unable to utilise a transfer pricing policy to give them protection either from other Group entities or market forces. The Group is bound together not by restrictive policies but more by the network formed by links between the internal audit and the accounting function which is interwoven throughout the organisation structure.

5.5 Questions

1. Identify the Group policy on decentralisation. Assess its strengths and weaknesses in achieving Group financial performance.
2. Evaluate the methods utilised by the Group to assess divisional performance.
3. *Watson and Baumler* (*Accounting Review*, July 1975) suggest that the need to achieve both decentralisation and integration goals in an organisation may be facilitated by the proper use of transfer pricing. Consider the position of Kimco identifying the needs for decentralisation and integration and compare their relative importance in this particular case.
4. Freely negotiated transfer prices may be set in such a way that they are dysfunctional. Identify how Kimco attempt to manage this problem.
5. Identify the roles performed by the internal audit unit. Examine how this set of roles contributes or detracts from the unit's ability to act as a control function within the organisation.
6. Discuss the advantages and potential dangers that may arise from the approaches to control adopted by Kimco giving particular attention to the position of the internal audit unit.

Note

1. Coates, J.B., Smith, J.E., Stacey, R.J., *Results of a Preliminary Survey into the Structure of Divisionalised Companies, Divisionalised Performance Appraisal and the Associated Role of Management Accounting*, CIMA Occasional Papers Series. August 1983.

6
Carcomp Foundries

6.1 Synopsis

The measurement of product profitability forms a substantial part of most management accounting texts, usually dealt with under topic heads, such as Total or Absorption Costing, Marginal, Direct, or Variable Costing, Cost Behaviour Analysis and Relevant Costs for Decision-Making. These measures have applications in tactical and strategic planning. The extent to which this textbook 'theory' is or is not applied by, or relevant to, practising accountants is a matter of continuing debate.

In many respects, this case study illustrates the adaption of textbook theory to practical challenges facing the company, the effects of which may run counter to readers' intuitive reactions. It examines the changing views of a product's profitability/viability within an organisation, as circumstances within the organisation and its industry change.

6.2 Background

The situation

The Alvar Group has a variety of diverse interests organised into Divisions, each with a number of operating units. This case relates to Carcomp Foundries Division, Alvar's foundry division, which had an operating unit (Harveys) devoted to the manufacture of cylinder heads, a cast iron motor component. Harveys comprised two specialised processes producing standard (SCH) and high-grade (HGCH) cylinder heads. The standard, made in the traditional manner, principally for one major motor company, was a relatively inferior product requiring further processing by the motor manufacturer, whereas the HGCH did not require this operation and was supplied to many British and overseas motor and commercial vehicle manufacturers. Each production process provided a good contribution and 'profit', as indeed did the whole operating unit.

6.3 Case details

Management accounting information systems

The division's management accounting information systems were based on a standard marginal costing system. Knowledge regarding cost behaviour is reflected in most routine management accounting documentation, considerable efforts having been taken to identify the most applicable classification for each element of cost, either in whole or part. Variable costs normally included:

- Direct materials including irrecoverable scrap and an allowance for returns from customers
- Direct labour
- Variable elements of indirect labour
  maintenance costs
  energy
  boxes

Operating statements concentrated on controllability, responsibility and attributability of incomes and expenditures, whether fixed or variable, variances being from flexed budgets.

There was a substantial awareness of the implications of cost behaviour and of the contribution concept, these being the bases of product cost and profitability information. Absorption/total product costs were produced for year-end accounts and some selling price decisions.

Product standards were based on prices and costs at the beginning of the year, although these could be updated to latest costs whenever required, as the computer cross-referenced purchase and other records with product standard information. Budgets incorporated expected adverse price/cost variances to adapt the 'known' standards at the beginning of the year to expected actual costs over the year.

Competition

The motor industry had shown a steady growth for many years. However, in the late 1970s/early 1980s the industry contracted substantially in the UK, Europe and worldwide. The derived demand for automotive iron casting production (including cylinder heads) followed a similar pattern (see Appendix 3), resulting in a substantial over-capacity in the industry and increasing significantly competition between producers both nationally and internationally.

Competition within the cylinder head market was exacerbated in 1979 when M & E Engineering, a manufacturer of motor components, entered the cylinder head market with the backing of one of Harveys' major customers. The resultant price and volume reductions naturally reduced the contribution and relative profitability of the Harveys cylinder head operation.

Reducing viability

The viability of the existing processes, originally conceived as a volume operation, had been seriously jeopardised. The longer-term view of the market was for a relatively small market size and share, and thus total sales volumes, in comparison with that which justified the existing plant, and, of course, at lower prices.

Management studies indicated that the cylinder head production operation remained viable even at the relatively small contribution levels, only because the existing plant had to be considered as a committed sunk cost.

Investment viability

During 1980 it became increasingly apparent that the capital equipment of the cylinder head operation was wearing out and would need to be replaced.

Bearing in mind the market forecasts, it was accepted that a replacement strategy would not be financially viable, and therefore alternative methods of production were sought which would provide a good-quality product at smaller volumes.

By late 1980, and after some considerable investigation, the most 'acceptable' production alternative was identified, which had a capital cost of £4m. However, appraised as a capital investment against the remaining/prospective products and customers, there was insufficient total contribution from all of the products, in spite of their individually positive contributions, to justify the £4m expenditure.

Alternatives

As the products made contributions, albeit lower ones than had previously been experienced, there was merit in seeking alternative methods of supplying the product from elsewhere within the company via the utilisation or adaptation of existing capacities. In particular, another of the division's operating units (Davidsons) was considered, as their existing machinery could accommodate cylinder head production, given only expenditure on tooling for which, in any event, the customer would normally pay. However, after detailed examination this was considered unviable, as Davidsons were already operating at or near their full capacity, and with existing products at a higher contribution per unit of capacity than that offered by the cylinder head products. Early in 1981, the decision was made to get out of the cylinder head business and close Harveys in spite of the product's positive and long-term contribution prospects.

M & E Engineering Co.

M & E had been attracted into cylinder head manufacture due to the low profitability of their existing motor component products and following the promise of substantial work by one of Harveys's major customers.

Whilst it had proved impossible to obtain direct confirmation of their considerations, it appears that M & E viewed this as a means of achieving some contribution towards their general establishment fixed costs, while using some existing under-utilised resources. It appears that M & E had been making losses and, although the additional work may have been expected to provide a turn-round, it is clear that the overall viability of M & E continued to be very doubtful indeed. Information from M & E on product profitability just did not exist, their lack of costing information apparently stemming from a lack of cost awareness and a belief that, if they charged market prices and made the product as efficiently as they could, they would make a profit. Unfortunately, it has not been possible to confirm this.

Briefly, only some one and a half years after the closure of Harveys cylinder head production, M & E made a trading loss in the seven months to April 1982 of £491,000 on sales of £1.767m. Whilst £158,000 of this was a depreciation charge, G P Engineering Group of which M & E was a part made a charge on M & E for loan interest (not included in the above figures) of £309,000 p.a., making a total loss of £800,000 in seven months (see Appendices 1 and 2). These losses, of course, reflected the contributions of all the products (including cylinder heads which represented one-third of total sales at this stage) set against company fixed costs. G P Engineering decided to close down the M & E operation and were interested predominantly in salvaging what they could from the wreckage.

Carcomp re-entry

Just prior to the Spring Bank Holiday of 1982, G P Engineering approached Harveys and two other companies with a view to their taking over all or part of the M & E operation. Over the long weekend the Carcomp's Financial and Managing Directors visited the M & E units to analyse available information and negotiate with G P Engineering. Obviously, M & E as a whole did not look attractive, their main assets being their possibly transitory customers for established products (tools being owned by the customers) and some reasonably good machinery, albeit some of little real value, together with the site on which the two factories stood.

Carcomp's initial reaction could well have been, 'Why re-enter a product market which only two years ago we considered unviable', when essentially circumstances had not changed, and the market was still depressed, with relatively low prices and high competition. However, circumstances within Carcomp had changed and, in particular, within their operating unit, Davidsons, which had previously rejected the cylinder head products. This unit was no longer at full capacity and would welcome new products which would bring contribution to pay for their existing long-term committed fixed costs. Thus, whilst the profitability of cylinder heads production had not changed, its potential position *vis-à-vis* Group capacity (i.e. Davidsons) and existing products had changed.

M & E was therefore viewed as a potentially attractive proposition, although not on a straight take-over basis.

For Carcomp and Davidsons, the questions were (a) what were the contributions of the M & E products, cylinder heads and other? (b) what were the long-term prospects for these products? (c) could they be fitted into the existing Davidsons operations and at what cost? and (d) would G P sell M & E's product and customer portfolio or insist on an 'all or nothing' package?

Detailed current product and operating costs were not maintained by M & E. However, cost and quantitative information on cylinder head products were available from the old Harveys operation, which were sufficient to estimate approximate contribution levels for most cylinder head products. These indicated that, whilst contributions on M & E products were certainly no better than they had been at Harveys, they were nevertheless significant enough to make a valuable contribution in total to Davidsons' fixed costs, even after the consideration of additional fixed assets which would be required. As many M & E customers were clamouring for Carcomp to take over their orders (due to Carcomp's reputation and, in many cases, their past relationships) this put tremendous pressure on M & E to sell quickly to Carcomp, in order to avoid losing a substantial part of the value of their business.

The deal

Carcomp were obviously in a position of strength in their dealings with G P Engineering and were, to a large extent, able to pick and choose from the bones of M & E. They agreed to 'buy' the product customer portfolio on a commission on sales basis, reducing after the first year and lasting only two years. This was partly due to the uncertain long-term prospects of customers staying with Davidsons, and the doubtful sales price and volume information provided by M & E. Carcomp also agreed to buy a few fixed assets to augment their facilities. This agreement was made by the two Carcomp Directors without formal referral to their main Board (see Appendix 1 for their subsequent report), following work done over the three days of the Spring Bank Holiday weekend.

As the directors' report shows (Appendix 1), a total of £3m of business was involved with an anticipated contribution of about £1m. It could be argued that this was confirmed by the M & E accounts (Appendix 2).

Davidsons' products

The change-over of production from M & E to Davidsons was organised over a weekend, with friendly relationships between the two companies, it being in G P's/M & E's interest to maintain sales. Tools were transported from M & E to Davidsons ready for a Monday start, to ensure continued production, the whole transfer causing little or no disruption to existing Davidsons production.

The additional M & E work, comprising cylinder head and other products, resulted in an increase of 40 per cent in the Davidsons' production tonnage and 50 per cent in sales value, although this represented only 30 per cent in terms of contribution. However, the addition resulted in an improved Davidsons' profit position of £700,000 per annum, half of which related to cylinder heads, when commission ceased to be payable. This figure was less than originally anticipated, due to a loss of M & E business during the change-over. Commission payable to G P during the first two years was about £150,000 and £75,000, respectively.

6.4 Appendix 1

To: Carcomp Foundries' Board
From: Finance Director

M & E ENGINEERING CO.

1. This company is a wholly owned subsidiary of G P Engineering Co. Due to excessive losses closure is to take place on 10 September 1982.

2. In spite of its title the company is only a foundry company producing cylinder heads and other motor components.

3. In the year ended 30 September 1981 it ran at a loss of £1,462,699.

4. So far the 1981/82 results are:

6 months to 31 March 1982.
April 1982

Sales value	£1,511,000	£256,000
Trading loss	£448,188	£43,414
Interest	£262,500	£46,250
Net loss	£710,688	£89,664
Including depreciation	£135,999	£22,666
Cash outflow	£574,689	£66,998

5. There are effectively two foundries, one producing only cylinder heads, but no analysis of results is available. In fact there is so little financial, costing or statistical information available that it is easy to see why the company cannot be managed. For instance, there is no attempt at product costs: 'We were just about to get round to it'. Some of the information in this report I obtained by adding up myself from source documents.

6. The following is an analysis of sales as up to date as possible:

	6 months to 31.3.82	*April and May 82*
Brake drums	534,781	193,141
Cylinder heads	501,946	104,468
Housings	100,388	10,563
Flywheels	230,721	107,163
Miscellaneous	116,439	12,494
Patterns	16,992	8,700
	£1,501,267	£436,529

By customer

	6 months to 31.3.82	*April and May 1982*
Car Manuf 1	678,535	275,561
Car Manuf 2	272,708	47,675
Car Manuf 3	386,544	79,553
Car Manuf 4	163,480	33,740
	£1,501,267	£436,529

7. There is no detailed tonnage analysis of these sales but I did manage to get first six months' good production figures – period 1–6:

Cyl hds	693	tonnes	£501,946	=	£724	tonne
Others	1932	tonnes	£982,329	=	£508	tonne
	2625	tonnes	£1484,275			

8. Scrap and Rejects were not available as a tonnage or percentage but only as sales value. Recent results of internal foundry scrap are as follows:

Week commencing	*Production sales value*	*Scrap sales value*	*%*
1.4.82	40,219	2,924	7.3
5.4.82	42,379	9,190	21.7
12.4.82	63,259	7,787	12.3
19.4.82	77,985	10,074	12.9
26.4.82	52,225	11,188	21.4
April total	£276,067	£41,163	14.9

Scrap in June is averaging 16.9%.

9. The reason for the high current demand for cylinder heads is that they had a furnace lining failure in May and produced no cylinder heads for nearly two weeks. Sales value of cylinder head production fell from an average of £80,000 per month to only £31,000.

10. Rejects for the six months to March were valued at £91,670 on casting sales of £1,484,275 = 6.2%.

11. Scrap and Rejects combined are therefore running in excess of 20%.

12. It was not possible to obtain prices of individual castings except for a few cylinder heads and brake drums which varied between £352 and £573 tonne.

13. So far as individual cyl. hds. are concerned, the following examples are for M & E compared with Harveys' prices at the time of cessation of trade:

Part No	*Harveys*	*M & E*	*Kgs.*	*£/tonne*
1269	3.491	3.716	5.45	681
1394	3.331	3.632	4.54	800
1414	2.092	3.504	5.00	700
1508	3.126	3.633	6.13	593
1510	4.199	6.730	10.68	630

All of the above are produced at four per box in a 42 × 20 × 7/7 and therefore averaging at least £14 box sales value. The company does not keep such statistics but an attempt to calculate the figure for the cyl. hd. foundry gave £87,925/5553 boxes = £15.80 box in February; £81,523/5697 = £14.30 in March, but these relate nett good sales after rejects with good boxes produced and therefore are not very reliable.

14. Clearly no financial guidance has been available to management to aid in running the operation.

15. The company was not prepared to reveal any figures relating to asset values but I did find that of the Balance Sheet value:

	£
Leasehold land and buildings	£400,000
New BMM line	1,100,000
Other items	900,000
	£2,400,000

16. The property is 4 acres leased until 2040 at a fixed rent of £7,122 per year.

17. The Ajax furnace is 42 tonnes capacity, 30 tonnes usable, but has a melt rate of only 2–3 tonnes per hour so that it uses a 12 hour night at off peak electricity rates. Keith says a new one would only cost £150,000, and Swindon would be interested in an August Sand Mill, a Multivac for

cleaning pits, and a small hanging shotblast plant.

18. Davidsons does not think much of the electric furnace on the cyl. hd. line and the manufacturer has gone out of business. There is a Eurocor Corebelter little used.

19. *What is likely to happen?*
It is quite clear that the company is of no value as a going concern but there must be profitable areas.

Canwell Foundries are to make an offer on Friday but presumably it is the non-cylinder head business they are after. The prices are very high for this class of work, but this will now change unless the deal is coupled with cylinder heads.

Farlow are, I understand, going to make an offer for the cylinder head business and the BMM new moulding line on Friday. They visited on Wednesday and have some engineers there today. This, I would say, is the main threat and could succeed.

Carcomp would appear to have little interest in the plant but would find the business useful, the annual rate being:

Cyl. hds.	£1.0m
Others	£2.0m
	£3.0m

which would produce about £1.0m additional contribution for the Division.

20. John Barry, the financial director of G P Engineering, is anxious to get as much below the line as possible. I suggested to him that an offer for the plant plus a percentage of sales acquired for the next year would give him the best solution. Accepting a lower offer for the plant would maximise his below the line write-off in the 1981/2 Accounts, but a commission on sales in 1982/3 would appear as a trading profit for the group. He said he might look favourably on such an arrangement.

Appendix 2
The financial statements of M & E Engineering Co.

M & E Engineering Co.
Operating statement for period to April 82

	Month			*Year to date*		
	Actual	*Budget*	*Variance*	*Actual*	*Budget*	*Variance*
Production	282,330	412,188		1,771,315	2,200,982	
Sales						
Patterns	1,150	—		18,142	-	
Castings	155,426	388,500		1,750,862	2,127,038	
Direct costs						
Materials	77,641	106,838		487,112	597,359	
WIP movement	(12,062)	(9,783)		92,224	(14,538)	
Patterns	3,169	1,000		28,481	7,000	
Electricity, etc.	33,270	25,778		276,597	218,778	
Direct labour	56,806	49,321		372,434	329,672	
Total	158,824	173,154		1,256,848	1,138,271	
Gross profit	97,752	215,346		512,156	988,767	
Overheads						
Works	93,614	87,908		656,727	596,289	
Maintenance	19,324	17,433		139,352	121,833	
Transport	6,940	8,250		60,048	48,450	
Admin	21,288	23,927		147,631	167,491	
Finance	46,250	46,417		308,750	324,917	
Total	187,416	183,935		1,312,508	1,258,980	
Profit prior to group	(89,664)	31,411		(800,352)	(270,213)	

Balance Sheet April 1982

		At 30.9.81		*At 30.4.82*
Fixed assets		2488631		2470910
Current assets				
Stock & WIP	526,125		432,251	
Debtors	584,799		449,595	
	1,110,924		881,846	
Current liabilities				
Bank overdraft	2,918,292		3,649,421	
Hire purchase	46,932		23,466	
Creditors	799,867		640,849	
	3,765,091		4,313,736	
Net current assets		(2,654,167)		(3,431,890)
Capital employed		(165,536)		(960,980)
Share capital		95,214		95,214
Reserves		(695,637)		(695,637)
Profit/loss 80/1		(1,462,699)		(1,462,699)
81/2		–		(800,352)
Group		1,897,586		1,902,494
Capital employed		(165,536)		(96,980)

Period to April 1982

	Month Actual	Month Budget	Month Variance	Year to Date Actual	Year to Date Budget	Year to Date Variance
Works overheads						
Salaries	10,974	13,250		78,762	92,750	
O/T premium staff	1,819	–		12,294	–	
Indirect wages	11,198	12,824		72,022	85,675	
O/T premium works	6,065	–		41,129	–	
Earnings related	13,667	12,562		89,536	85,847	
Holiday pay, etc.	8,459	6,833		55,346	47,833	
Waste disposal	2,224	1,700		16,500	11,800	
Fettling shop supplies	2,736	2,720		23,032	18,880	
Welding mats	528	425		3,867	2,950	
General consumables	5,835	7,595		51,623	40,556	
Equipment hire	5,726	5,000		39,375	35,000	
Moulding box repairs	153	333		1,792	2,333	
Canteen	1,164	750		9,323	5,250	
Training	400	1,250		3,461	8,750	
Depreciation	22,666	22,666		158,665	158,665	
Total	93,614	87,908		656,727	596,289	
Maintenance overheads						
Plant repairs	13,951	10,000		101,745	70,000	
Wages	5,373	7,433		37,607	51,833	
Total	19,324	17,433		139,352	121,833	
Transport overheads						
Haulage	4,748	35,662				
Vehicle maintenance	191	5,675		7,448	30,850	
Wages	1,251	1,825		11,688	12,350	
Depreciation	750	750		5,250	5,250	
Total	6,940	8,250		60,048	48,450	
Admin overheads						
Salaries and pensions	5,822	7,083		40,924	29,583	
Travel, entertaining	1,526	833		8,796	5,833	
Legal and audit costs	600	1,417		4,311	9,917	
Postage and telephone	943	667		6,682	4,667	
Printing and stationery	70	83		775	583	
HP interest	1,083	1,083		7,583	7,583	
Group service charge	–	–		–	–	
Rent	594	594		4,158	4,158	
Rates	5,000	5,250		35,001	36,750	
Insurance	4,200	4,750		29,400	33,250	
Office expenses	1,450	2,167		10,001	15,167	
Total	21,288	23,927		147,631	167,491	
Finance overheads						
Bank interest/charges	46,250	46,417		308,750	324,917	

Appendix 3

Comparison of UK vehicle production with iron castings output 1975–1982

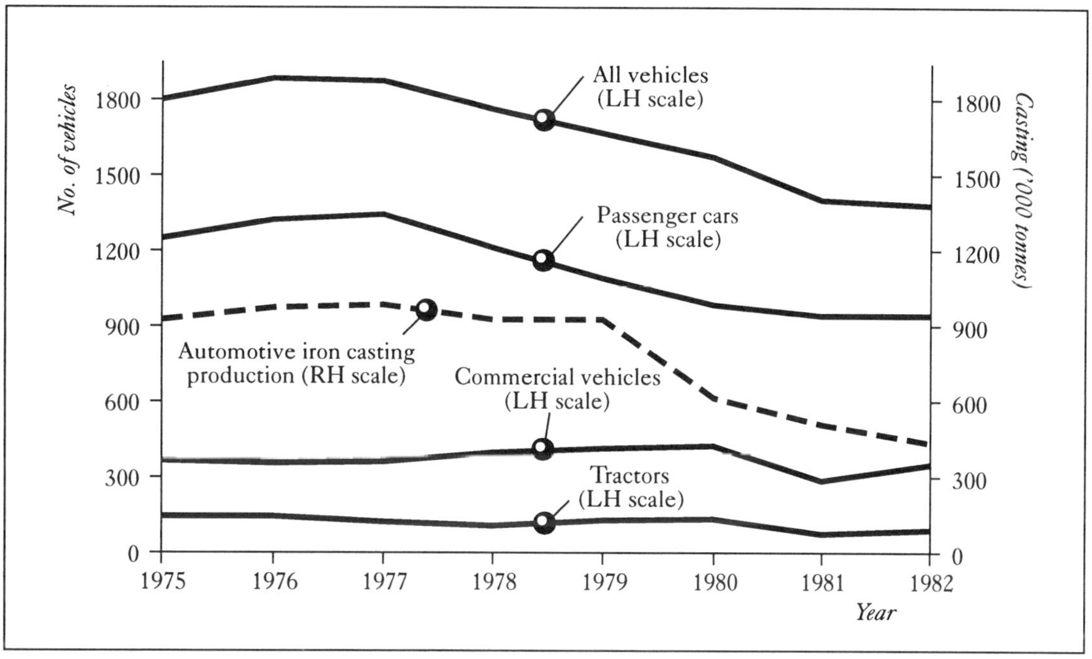

6.5 *Questions*

1. Is the cylinder head product 'profitable'? Discuss.

2. What is the role of accounting measures of profitability in strategic decisions and, in particular, helping to identify a product's position within its life cycle and the Boston Consulting Group Matrix? Where and for what reasons would you place cylinder heads within these strategic frameworks? How does this conflict with the evidence on profitability in this case?

3. What information would you have sought to help you decide:

   (a) whether or not to continue manufacture of cylinder heads within Harveys as the market size and share declined,
   (b) whether or not to continue manufacture when Harveys' plant needed replacing,
   (c) whether or not to buy the customer portfolio from G P Engineering and if so, the price to pay?

4. The product portfolio effect can be viewed as having a similar basis to the concept of 'economic scope' identified by *Manes, Chen and Greenburg* (*Cost Volume Profit Analysis for the Multi-product Firm*, 1984) relating to 'the situation where two or more products can be produced with less cost by one firm than two or more firms separately'. These economies, they suggested, would result from:

   (1) production complementarity for inputs of one or more variable factors of production, and
   (2) the existence of common or shared fixed factors of production.

   Examine this view.

5. In the light of this case, how valuable is knowledge regarding product profit and contribution levels?

6. Consider the arguments for and against the suggestion that Davidsons were wrong (a) to reject the cylinder head business on the closure of Harveys, and (b) to accept it on the closure of M & E.

7. In the situation faced by Carcomp's management, how would you place a value on a customer/product portfolio? What are the factors, strategic and tactical, you would need to consider and evaluate in this situation?

8. How important was the method by which Carcomp paid for the customer portfolio?

7
Eastcote

7.1 Synopsis

An understanding of the manner in which cost can be expected to respond to proposed actions is a central element in the preparation and use of financial information for decision-making purposes. Indirect costs may be considered no less interesting than direct manufacturing costs in the context of modern manufacturing technology. A simple classification of cost into fixed and variable elements is likely to be inappropriate for decision-making purposes if the relationship between volume and cost varies both in a non-linear manner and with the time horizon over which the cost levels can be adjusted.

This case reports how a company recognised this problem and went on to attempt to identify and explain the cost/volume relationship it perceived. It examines a situation in which a company was concerned initially to generate information relevant to the evaluation of contraction policies. For this situation it was recognised that the variable costs, used in the company's ongoing management accounting, were intended for decisions over a shorter time horizon than was required. Even within short-term horizons the effects on cost of contraction were considered to differ from those of expansion. The range of considerations went beyond those where linearity was a sufficient approximation to a non-linear function.

The manner in which the company approached these problems are examined, making use of their own identification of how the alternative descriptions of cost behaviour may have implications for routine management accounting. The focus of attention in this case is the identification of non-linear cost behaviour within a service department and its importance for divisional decisions and control.

7.2 Background

The company

The company, a wholly owned subsidiary within a major group, is treated by the holding company as a separate division producing a range of high-volume domestic consumer products supplied mainly to supermarket and other retail chains as well as wholesale distributors. The performance of the division was formerly evaluated on the basis of two major indicators. The first of these was return on assets, an indicator that had been employed for a considerable period of time. This was calculated as the ratio of historic cost accounting profit before tax and interest to operating assets, the latter being measured by the book value of fixed and current assets excluding cash net of current liabilities. The other indicator, 'divisional cash flow', was introduced only three years before this study, and was found by adding back depreciation to trading profit and deducting increases in operating fixed assets. Both these indicators were evaluated by a comparison with the forecast produced by an annual strategic review. These key indicators were reported on a four-weekly cycle, the particular form of presentation or breakdown of the data being at the discretion of the division.

Although the holding company only required this data on a regular basis, requests were made in addition for ad hoc financial information. In conjunction with the introduction of divisional cash flow as a performance measure, some emphasis has been placed on presentation of additional data in a form consistent with the net present value approach to decision-making.

Internal organisation

Within the divisional company further decentralisation is to be found: divisional responsibilities are split into eight major operating units plus a small number of other commercial units and divisional central service departments. Operating units are assessed by a comparison with budget of an analysis of trading profit net of overheads for the unit. Transfers between operating units are made with internal prices determined by negotiation between units but within explicit limits based on cost. Service departments are treated as cost centres and the costs incurred by these departments, which contribute to operating unit overheads, are charged by initially apportioning budgeted cost on the basis of sales value and making adjustments at the year end for realised differences between budget and actual.

The environment

Although some of the products of this division are market leaders and many of the others are major brands, competition is fierce. The division's customers compete keenly in the High Street; alternative brands are usually available; the high volume of purchases made by major customers gives them considerable bargaining power in the market.

As a result, pricing policies for each product line are regularly reviewed and cost information is a valuable input into the pricing process. It is also noteworthy that rising real interest rates and the effects of recent recession had been causes of concern for group management who were endeavouring to achieve improved returns and levels of efficiency.

Treatment of cost and cost control

The overhaul of the management accounting system that had introduced cash flow reporting and emphasis on net present value was associated with the introduction of a marginal cost/contribution format for the presentation of cost information. This was achieved by deducting direct costs and traceable overheads from sales value to give a contribution figure in addition to the trading profit figure for each business unit. As a result, a form of variable cost as well as full cost information was available to the operating units. Attempts were made to distinguish between the fixed and variable components of the cost of service departments, and there was some interest in attempting to move from the position where these service departments were all treated as cost centres to one where they were also profit centres. Particular focus is placed on selling and distribution costs which comprise about 8 per cent of total costs. Major difficulties had been recognised in establishing charge-out rates which would both provide an incentive for the service unit and yet not be so high that it led to significant distortion of the marginal costs of products.

7.3 Case details

Initial phase

In response to group demands, evaluations were undertaken to consider how divisional performance could be improved by making cutbacks. Examination was undertaken first of the effects of modest cutbacks and, subsequently, of more substantial cutbacks of the order of twice the turnover reduction. It was the apparent inconsistency of the results obtained from these evaluations that led to a recognition of the nature and importance of the behaviour of selling and distribution costs, which is the focus of this case.

In attempting to identify possible savings from modest cutbacks, attention was given to the effect of eliminating the activities with the lowest return on assets. Although a group of products could be identified which had returns, calculated on existing bases, below that required, the effects of shut-down of the operations of the operating unit responsible for the production and packing of products would have led to a decline in the division's performance. This in itself was not altogether surprising, since the evaluation had made efforts to identify relevant costs, i.e. costs that would change, rather than just using the cost classifications used in regular reporting. For selling and distribution costs, in particular, the effects of the cutback would make little difference, inferring that the marginal cost savings were low. At this stage, the evaluation considered the overall cost position with and without the products under examination. Careful attention was given to the manner in which activities would be carried out in the continuing operations. The exercise was intended to try to obtain an understanding of the cost/volume relationship which applied to this category of cost.

The routine treatment of selling and distribution costs, charging them to all operating units on the basis of equal rates, was not adopted here. The approach may be described as identifying the attributable costs of the threatened products; it would be consistent with using Shillinglaw's definition of attributable cost[1] as that which 'could be avoided, on the average, if a product or function were discontinued entirely without changing the supporting organisation structure'. The inclusion of apportioned selling and distribution costs in the calculation of trading profit for an operating unit may be seen to be an over-statement of the attributable costs.

What was perhaps more interesting, however, was that these results were not borne out when considering the effects of a substantial cutback. Extending the range of activities to be terminated by including a second group of products (being those with the next lowest returns) showed a modest improvement in divisional performance.

A simple answer to this apparent conflict might have been that the ranking provided by return on assets had given the wrong priority, and that preference should have been given to eliminating the second group of products rather than those in the initial group. However, this was examined and found not to be the case. Comparison of the alternative projections were more revealing, showing that the effects on selling and distribution and other costs, which were relatively unchanged by modest cutback, were significant in the case of substantial cutback. The nature of these cost changes was clearly one of interest in this business.

Further investigations were undertaken by the division to improve their understanding of this particular feature of their operations. It was evident that the various services could be provided by a whole range of methods each having a different mix of fixed and variable cost. As the level of activity expanded so it would be preferable to move from a method involving low fixed costs and high variable costs to one with relatively higher fixed costs and lower variable costs. A breakeven point of the form illustrated at point V in Figure 1 would occur at which it would be preferable to change method. In Figure 1, XVY represents the cost of supply of the service using a method (Method I) having relatively low fixed costs (OX) and an alternative (Method II) is represented by WVZ. Only at volumes below that indicated at point V is Method I preferred to Method II, V being the breakeven point. The cumulative effect of the change arising from a series of such breakeven points is illustrated by Figure 2 and shows that, although short-run fluctuations in volume within a limited range may be adequately represented by a straight line, in the longer run, over a wider range, a curve would be more appropriate.

In the case of distribution services a number of stages can be readily identified as volume is reduced:

- an organisation with a major national distribution network with a fleet of vans making deliveries from production locations to depots, and depots to customers;
- the elimination of some of the fleet and depots until a single depot remains;
- reduction to a basic fleet with short-term hiring arrangements to meet particular needs and combining an in-house service with the use of external carriers.

Identifying cost changes

The divisional management was concerned to pursue further the nature of the relationship between cost and volume of these service costs, giving particular attention to selling and distribution costs. Already they had carried out studies which had produced projections of the costs of the distribution function at two levels of operation, in addition to the existing level. Further, it was not difficult to derive additional components of the projected cost behaviour function. The first effected the condition that complete shutdown of the whole division would be associated with the complete elimination of selling and distribution costs in the long run. The second utilised cost information relating to the charges that would be made by outside carriers; this information was already being collected to establish the viability of keeping rather than abandoning the in-house distribution function.

The information available enabled four points to be established on the long-run cost/volume, further represented by cost at existing, modest cutback, substantial cutback and shutdown volumes of activity. Taken with the external prices, which indicated the initial cost of expansion from zero output, an attempt could be made to identify a suitable curve to fix the points, and this was attempted by inspection. The suggestion that the rate of saving increased in proportion to the amount of cutback provided a fit acceptable to divisional management. This relationship could be re-expressed as: 'the percentage cost saving is the square of the percentage cutback'.[2]

Interpretation and implications

Management set out to explain the profit changes they had observed in their examination of possible cutback options. In a similar way to the manner in which the marginal costs decline, the net revenue that can be earned from expansion of volume can also be ranked. Given that the decision to include a particular product in the range is relatively independent of the choice of other products, those with the highest net revenue would be selected for production first, priority reducing with the net revenue. Figure 3 presents a simplified illustration of the resulting position in which there are only three products and assuming that the relationship between net revenue and volume for each product can be represented by a straight line. The competition between suppliers in this industry means that this assumption was regarded as not unreasonable for all but the lowest volumes of output of a product.

An examination of Figure 3 provides some insight into the results identified by this division when viewing its plans. The initial profit is given by the excess of net revenue over selling and distribution costs shown as AB in Figure 3. The slope of net revenue per unit for product 3 (AC) is flatter than the others in a cutback. If distribution costs are allocated to products in direct relationship to the volume measure then, if AC is flatter than BE, product 3 would be earning negative trading profits (given by CE – AB). However, if modest cutback by eliminating product 3 to achieve a volume shown as P_m were undertaken net revenue would decline along AC, but selling and distribution costs would only decline to point D. It can be seen that this produces an overall reduction in revenue for the division where CD is greater than AB.

More substantial cutback by eliminating product 2 and reducing output to P_s may not be justified by examining the trading profit results where CE is greater than FH. Nevertheless, the effective change in costs compatible with net revenue shown as F would be a shift to G. It is quite possible for the resulting divisional profit (FG) to be less than that at CD and even AB. In this way substantial cutback may be worthwhile, even though modest cutback eliminating only those products which are relatively less attractive may not be worthwhile.

Further considerations

Having identified the nature of the cost behaviour in this case, the divisional management wished to see how they might make use of this information. Two general points readily emerge.

First, it can be seen that some products could be described as 'riding on the back' of others. These others bring the scale of operations up to a level where advantage can be taken of lower marginal costs resulting from higher fixed cost but lower variable cost. In this way product 3 in the illustration would not be worthwhile unless there were existing operations which brought production levels up to a level of about P_m. In fact, this effect can produce conditions of mutual independence between products. Take the case illustrated in Figure 3. Here, the products 1, 2, 3 taken together produce a profit shown by AB in the diagram. In this case:

AB > FG > CD

Consider the position at output P_S. Since FG > CD a direct evaluation would indicate that product 2 was not worthwhile. However, it can be seen that taken in combination with product 3, which itself is inferior to product 2, it is worthwhile expanding. In this case the division were encouraged from their results to identify ways in which expansion rather than contraction could improve their overall performance, taking advantage of the low marginal costs of the relevant services.

A second feature of this cost behaviour can also be observed. It concerns the importance of the current level of output in determining future changes, particularly in the short term. In expressing the relationship between cost and output in mathematical form the range of the function was limited to those volumes between zero and the existing level of output. Clearly, point B on the selling and distribution cost curve represents a point of discontinuity so that further expansion beyond P_0 would not lead to a decline in cost, as indicated by the equation. Cutback would initially produce only small savings in the short term since many of the fixed costs would be unavoidable over this horizon. Only in the longer term could travel be made along the curve from B towards O.

Of subsequent concern to divisional management has been the implications of this cost function for transfer pricing. The existing treatment of the selling and distribution departments as cost centres, and the allocation of these costs to operating units on the basis of equal charge for equal volume, effectively treats these costs as if they fitted along the straight line OHEB in Figure 3. The approach can be criticised for its failure to charge at marginal cost. However, it does allow the department to cover its total costs. This would not be achieved using marginal cost, which is close to zero at the existing level of operations.

7.4 Concluding remarks

The specific attention, given in this case, to take into account aspects of cost behaviour often ignored, offers an indication of the practical importance of these aspects. The perception of the relationship between cost and volume of activity is seen to be dependent upon the time horizon over which change is considered to occur, and both the extent and direction of such change. These factors cannot be ignored in the measurement of cost behaviour. Here external information, in the form of the current prices for varying ways of providing the required services, are integrated within calculations based on perceived inputs at different levels of activity.

The explicit recognition of non-linearity in cost/volume relationships directs attention to the implications of the resulting varying marginal cost. One aspect is the transfer pricing considerations of the subject company. Decisions are distorted by the use of an average cost which exceeds marginal cost. The use of a service capacity by a range of products, which results in providing the service at lower cost than separate provision, has particular significance for management accounting. The products take on some of the properties of joint products, with both their inherent accounting problems and commercial advantages.

The set of products may be able to co-exist profitably even though none of them is financially viable alone. This is not unlike the advantages often attributed to 'synergy'. This represents a potential relative advantage over attempts to compete without taking on a full range of products.

From the management accounting point of view, identifying service costs to particular products becomes subject to the criticisms of joint costing methods. It may be essential, as in the consideration of product elimination in this case, to examine the effects on the total range of products for decisions apparently concerning only one product. The context in which the product operations are undertaken becomes especially relevant.

Despite the low marginal costs that may exist at volumes of activity close to existing levels, the viability of the portfolio of products depends on some products generating revenues which contribute sufficient in excess of these marginal costs, to cover the non-marginal service costs. Control of performance needs to ensure that this is achieved, and this poses further problems for management accounting. Different products will be expected to produce different contributions over and above marginal cost.

If this was to be embodied in the transfer prices of a decentralised organisation it would appear to imply different prices being charged to different products in a manner somewhat related to 'ability to pay'.

The use of a range of transfer prices for the supply of the same service for different products is likely to be difficult to justify to product managers, especially those responsible for products facing the higher transfer prices. Nevertheless, continuing to use an orthodox average cost based transfer may not only fail to exploit the potential of the more profitable products, but prevent more marginal but nevertheless beneficial lines from ever emerging. Over-simplification in management accounting may obscure such management problems but may also lead to management accounting being considered irrelevant to the reality with which it is concerned. By contrast, the company in this case has brought important complexities into its considerations.

Figure 1

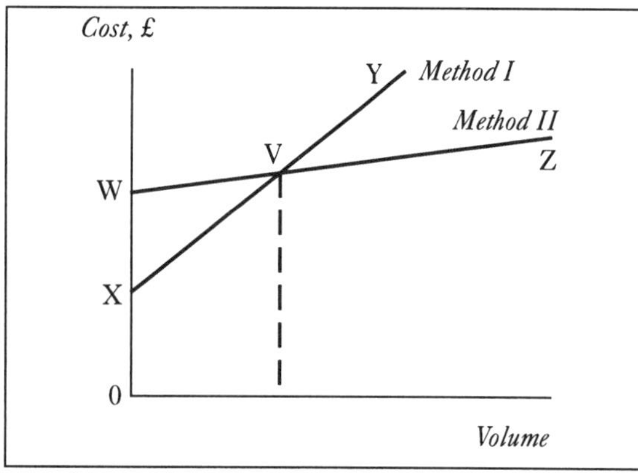

Figure 2

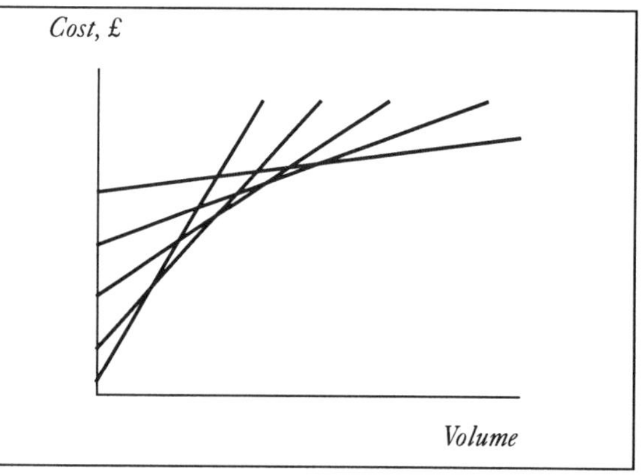

Figure 3

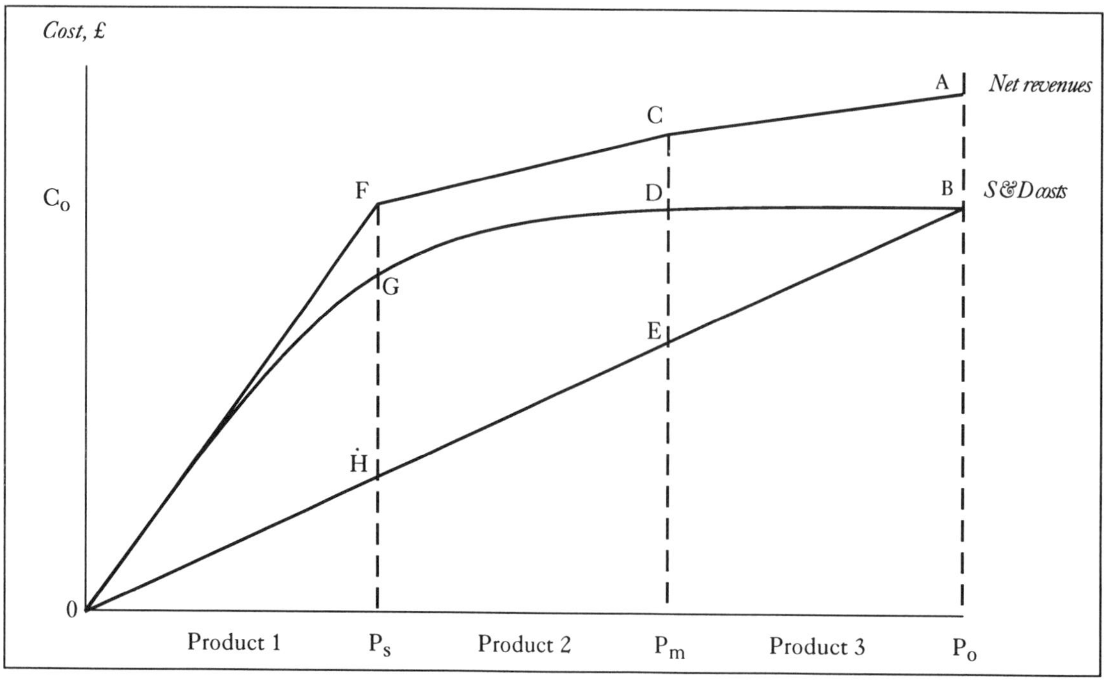

7.5 Questions

1. Explain what is meant by the concept of attributable costs. What types of decisions might make use of the concept?

2. It has been argued that all costs are variable in the long run, and fixed in the short run. Examine how changes in time horizons might be expected to change the view taken of cost behaviour. What implications could this have for responsibility accounting?

3. Explain the relationship between traditional cost-volume-profit analysis and the breakeven charts produced for Eastcote.

4. The use of average cost as a surrogate for marginal cost may prevent taking advantage of 'product synergy'. Explain how Eastcote has tried to overcome this problem. What implications does this have for product portfolios?

5. Eastcote has given some consideration to adopting an overhead charge-out policy which charges different costs to different products in a manner related to 'ability to pay'.

- Explain the reasons for supporting such charge-out policy.
- Discuss the difficulties of operating the policy.
- Examine how a two-part tariff approach charging a fixed lump sum amount plus variable costs charged at a constant amount per unit might operate in the circumstances faced by Eastcote.

Note

1 See *G. Shillinglaw*, 'The concept of attributable cost', *Journal of Accounting Research*, Spring 1963.

2 In mathematical form:

$$C_p = \left[2 \left\{ \frac{P}{P_0} \right\} - \left\{ \frac{P}{P_0} \right\}^2 \right] \times C_0$$

$$\text{for } 0 \leq P \leq P_0$$

Where C_0 = existing level of cost
C_p = level of cost at output P
P_0 = existing level of output

8
Midland Metals

8.1 Synopsis

The following examines the concepts of fixity and variability in costs adopted by the company, the ways in which these have been quantified, and the use of management accounting information by the company in tendering for new products and in general product pricing.

8.2 Background

The company

Midland Metals is a group of engineering companies, each company operating in broadly the same sector of industry as the others, but utilising different manufacturing processes. The management accounting system employed within the Group is described by the Financial Director as 'a marginal costing approach', although it is possible to extract both absorption and marginal cost information.

8.3 Case details

The management accounting system

Appendix A – the Standard Cost Schedule – illustrates the way in which cost is analysed in the short-term budgets and departmental operating statements throughout the Group. The cost breakdown into variable, semi-variable and fixed is classic in its alignment with textbook expectations of a system which aims to provide marginal cost information.

Excluding direct materials, costs defined as variable typically account for 50 per cent of total cost, and 'variability', either entirely or partially, extends to well over half the individual cost items within one of the manufacturing companies.

Detailed product/department costing with the usual allocations and apportionments is carried out through the manufacturing line to Central Manufacture as illustrated below. The latter consists of those expense items which cannot be directly allocated to factory units. Similarly, there are accounts for the individual factory units for expenses which cannot be directly allocated to processes. These costs are ultimately assigned to process accounts via a series of apportionments. It is interesting to note that the variable, semi-variable, fixed cost classification is maintained in the budgets of the Central Manufacture and factory accounts. In theory, a marginal cost may be defined for total manufacturing cost, though it is a figure which will contain cost apportionments.

Figure 1

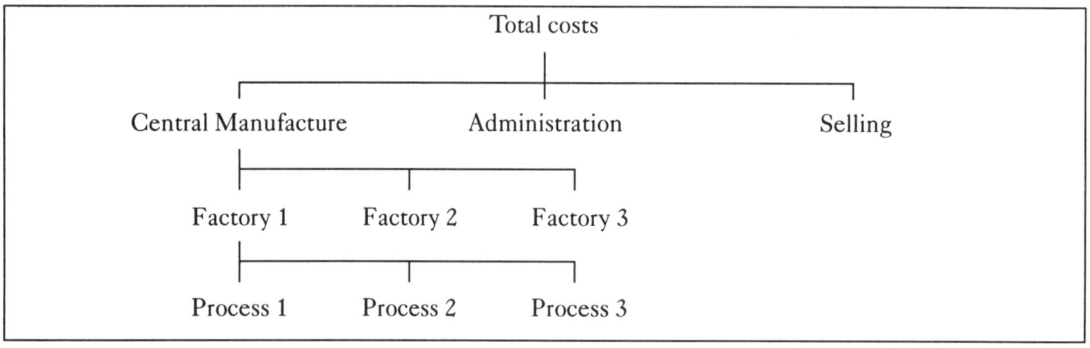

With respect to the individual items of expense, they represent a list which would be typical of items which would be found in a very wide range of engineering industry. Their treatment in these accounts owes a great deal to the value placed by management on receiving marginal cost information, though without there being any unquestioning belief that it is the cure for all problems or that it can always be applied even in circumstances in which it would be apparently appropriate.

Cost behaviour analysis

Regression analysis had been tried in a number of cases, but the results had been unsatisfactory: those obtained were either misleading in the context of known future changes or even gave answers which did not really explain the existing situation. At present, cost variability is largely assessed on the basis of experience moderated by circumstantial factors.

Other than material, the principal process cost which is treated as variable is *direct labour*. In spite of the fact that it is often commented that direct labour is a fixed short-term expense in most cases today, the ability to vary this cost in this case is achievable realistically, at least within a restricted range of movement of total output. The range quoted is plus 10 per cent to minus 20 per cent of the current output level. Diagrammatically the situation may be represented as:

Figure 2

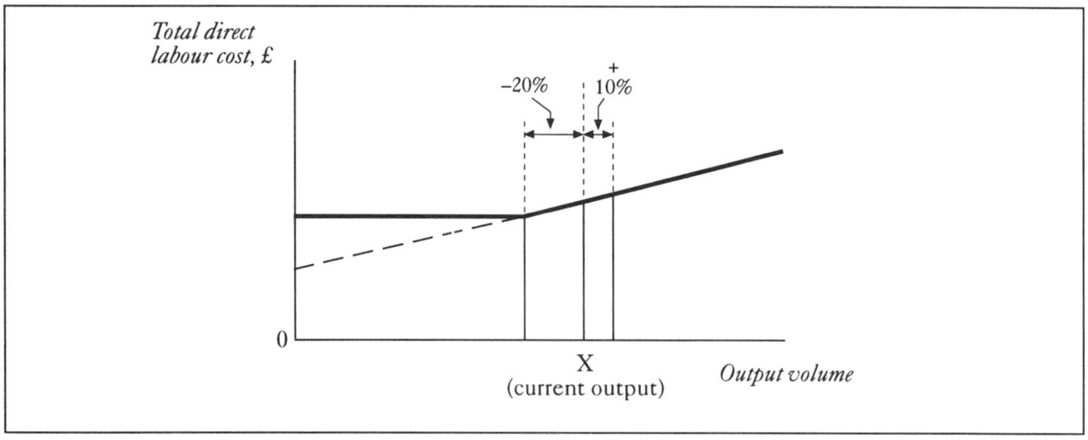

Below a 20 per cent contraction in output, the current direct labour force cost would indeed become fixed, while above plus 10 per cent consideration has to be given to overtime (the overtime premium being included in a separate budget) and to higher levels still, to introducing a further shift.

There is thus a considerable range in output in which direct labour can be regarded as variable and controllable. It is justified as follows:

(a) Lay-offs to a four-day week (from the current five-day) could be obtained without difficulty and with union agreement.
(b) Work is scheduled so that the first lay-off day is, say, Friday of the first week and Monday of the second, thus enabling unemployment benefit to be claimed. This substantially obviates worker resentment at losing money as a result of lay-offs.
(c) At the upper end of the scale, there is strong management reluctance to introduce a second shift, so that on occasion working weeks of up to 75 hours have been recorded for direct labour over an extended period, rather than introduce the greater rigidity in cost control imposed by introducing two shifts.
(d) The incentive element in pay is substantial so that guaranteed-week basic pay is certain to be exceeded in the course of normal working of current production schedules.

The concept of relevant range is frequently quoted in management accounting texts, and this case serves to illustrate clearly that below the maximum reduction, direct labour would certainly tend to become a fixed expense. The dotted line on the diagram is a notional and spurious representation of the variability of direct labour cost. Definition of the range is dependent on very specific circumstances, with a degree of uniqueness likely in all cases.

Other costs attributed as being wholly Variable (V) or partly, Semi-variable (SV), in the short-term period were:

General shop labour	(V)
'Process' labour	(SV)
Overtime and shift allowance – direct	(V)
Tool cleaning	(V)
Overtime and shift allowance – indirect	(V)
Consumable stores	(V)
Small tools	(V)
Process materials	(V)
Tool maintenance	(SV)
Other process tools	(SV)

Electricity, gas and gas oil are central costs, treated as semi-variable. The central costs themselves when finally apportioned to production departments retain their fixed/variable classification in department budgets, but principally for product costing rather than budgeting purposes.

Formal analysis of cost variability using regression techniques had been tried, but not successfully. In practice, the best that could be achieved was to use experience to attest to a cost item being likely to vary to some degree with volume changes, and then to budget the expected expenditures in relation to expected activity. Thus, variable cost per unit is simply expenditure divided by activity. Relevant range considerations are much less definite in these cases and the impression is gained that a considerable degree of tolerance must be permitted in cost control (variance) interpretations. Electricity might normally be considered a good candidate for formal statistical cost analysis but, due to the fact that direct measurement of cost with output could not be carried out, produced only fair regression results, no better than could be obtained via rather more simple methods.

The unit variable element of overtime, i.e. the overtime premium, at agreed rates, is treated as being a variable cost.

Management interpretation of cost behaviour

The way cost is classified in cases where there is considerable doubt as to its fixity and variability is interesting. Attention is given to obtaining the 'right response' from managers with expenditure responsibility. This is considered best attained by labelling expenses 'variable' wherever there is reasonable doubt as to whether it is really variable or fixed. Management believe that the psychology of the case for approaching the problem this way is that to call a cost 'fixed' invites the response that there is little which can be done to control it in the short term. Even if one could reasonably suspect fixity, approaching the problem this way puts pressure on managers to improve efficiency so as to be able to show expected cost savings in adverse conditions. However, there are obvious problems in having to employ a reinterpretation if activity levels are rising. Over the past few years with the strong tendency to contraction experienced in this industry, the weight of advantage in these cases has been to apply the 'variable' cost label. Little adverse reaction has been reported from managers whose spending budgets have been controlled – at least in part – this way.

Management accounting data in pricing decisions

There are two distinct pricing problems within the company:

(a) Repeat orders for smaller products, purchased in relatively high volumes, requiring non-special production facilities.
(b) Orders for products on a long-term contract basis, involving possibly a research and development phase, and acquisition of specialised, dedicated production equipment.

Management believe that, for the former orders (a), the availability of the kind of information generated by the management accounting function and described above would be appropriate to the requirements of tactical short-term pricing. However, only total absorption product cost data is provided to line sales managers. With the longer term case (b), where there is the possibility of a contract period of up to ten years ahead, the information needs change entirely and pricing policy is much more related to an evaluation of the contract using discounted cash flow appraisals.

Long-term contract pricing

The facilities created in the circumstances of (b) above are specific to the production of a model by a particular manufacturer, and once a contract is signed both customer and supplier are committed to each other for an extended period.

The company stands to lose on the prototype manufacture, which is an expensive process, if a contract bid is finally unsuccessful. However, in both cases – prototype and final manufacture – cost estimates have to be prepared on a unique basis, without using routinely prepared management accounting information. There are, of course, intermediate cases where facilities may have to be enhanced in some way or other, for example when original order quantities are being increased, thereby requiring additional production capacity.

All costs attributable directly to the acceptance of a contract must be recovered over the contract life.

Two points are worthy of note:

(i) that the overall evaluation of the process requires the accounting function to quote *three* measures:

- undiscounted payback;
- accounting rate of return;
- DCF (internal rate of return).

Inflation adjustments are added on a very broad basis to both costs and revenues: 'broad' meaning that not all elements of cost are individually estimated. Since the accounting rate of return (return on capital employed) is used within the company as a performance measure, management consider it should also be applied to project evaluation.

However, this presents difficulties for reconciliation of actual returns against the originally projected return. The latter is quoted as an average over the life of the asset (average revenue over average capital employed). The actual annual figure may depart substantially from this.

Given a project coming on stream in Year 3 (i.e. after the research and development phase) and thereafter producing a constant sales volume and earning a constant gross margin, the average accounting rate of return (ROCE) would be around 24.4 per cent ($^{85.6}/_{350}$). The actual annual ROCE figures differ markedly, rising due to the effect of increasing depreciation:

Year	*1*	*2*	*3*	*4*	*5*	*6*	*7*	*8*	*9*	*10*
Net profit (£000)	—	—	107	107	107	107	107	107	107	107
Capital employed (£000)	210	190	636	566	496	426	356	286	216	146
ROCE (%)	—	—	16.8	18.9	21.2	25.1	30.0	37.4	49.5	75.2

(ii) that product cost figures are provided for investment appraisals along the lines of the standard management accounts, i.e.:

- total product cost, current level
- marginal product cost, current level

If the estimates have to be changed, the incremental costs involved would be shown as a separate figure added to the original estimates.

Once the products are treatable as current production items, they will bear an absorption of general overheads not specifically related to the above information.

8.4 *Concluding remarks*

The great majority of the company's work involving the question of pricing comes in the short-term category. However, in terms of the proportion of total turnover affected by pricing decisions, the long-term contract category ultimately provides a very significant amount of business to the company.

8.5 *Questions*

1. Discuss whether any practical purposes are served by the apportionment of central expenses to individual operating units.

2. Examine the use of regression analysis for the purpose of quantifying cost relationships.

   For what reasons might it be believed that regression analysis does not provide as meaningful information as could be produced by deliberations based upon managerial judgement and experience?

3. Identify the reasons why labour might be considered as a fixed or variable cost by organisations in the short term.

4. What are the respective roles of cost behaviour analysis and absorption costing techniques in pricing decisions?

5. Do you consider that a ROCE calculation is useful to the evaluation of long-term capital investment projects? Is it possible to reconcile such a calculation with a DCF-based appraisal?

6. What difficulties may be experienced for annual management performance appraisal based on ROCE, when investment decisions are based on DCF?

Appendix

Standard expense schedule

Company
Division | Date | Department | Dept. code

Title	*No.*	*Class*	*Amount*	*Rate /hr.*	*No. of workers*	*Hours*	*Rate /hr.*	*Amount*	*Amount*
Direct Labour:									
Machine 1		V	1,720		4	624		1,720	
Machine 2		V	4,180		8	1,266		4,180	
Management and supervision		C						3,560	3,560
General shop labour		V	480					480	
Process labour		SV	3,040					3,360	320
O/T and shift premium allowance (direct)		V	1,200					1,700	
Tool cleaning and coating		V	1,700					1,200	
O/T and shift premium allowance (indirect)		V	1,660					1,660	
Rectification		C						80	80
Consumable stores		V	340					340	
Small tools		V	60					60	
Process materials		V	6,220					6,220	
Maintenance plant: labour		C						2,220	2,220
materials		C						1,340	1,340
Other process material		V	600					600	
Tool maintenance		SV	2,900					5,800	2,900
Other process tools		SV	80					260	180
			17,780					28,380	10,600
Centre overhead			23,302					69,758	46,456
			46,982					104,038	57,056
Direct materials		V	169,450					169,450	

Account class | Approvals | Date Effective

V = Variable
SV = Semi-variable
C = Constant (fixed)

9
Stapylton A

9.1 Synopsis

Stapylton A is one of two distinct studies based on the single company, Stapylton. The general background to the company is given in this particular case but, of course, is common to both.

Stapylton A deals with the introduction of a new management accounting reporting system, which aims at the substitution of attribution and management of costs for a previous system based on routinely administered absorption costing. A new management accountant had taken over who felt that the latter costing, whilst having to be recognised for certain purposes, was of little value in a dynamic business in a competitive environment.

The case describes the new reporting system and how it relates to business segments. It also covers the planning cycle, its evaluation and the level of details in cost analysis.

On the basis of the case, questions are related to business segmentation, cost behaviour, cost analysis and the concept of managed costs. Readers may also reflect on steps the company has taken towards an activity-based type of cost analysis.

9.2 Background

The situation

Concern with the poor performance of Western manufacturing industry compared in particular with Japanese success has been the source of a series of criticisms of traditional management accounting *(Cooper,* 1989; *Johnson and Kaplan*, 1987; *Cooper and Kaplan*, 1987). A number of US writers have advocated a major change in management accounting practice which would give significant major emphasis to activity-based costing.

Bromwich and Bhimani (1989) consider the changes advocated to be of relatively limited value on their own. In particular, it is suggested they may over-emphasise short-term operational management to the neglect of the strategic dimension which recognises the pertinent competitive context: 'there is a need for management accounting to become more externally focused to enable the enterprise to look outwards to the final goods market'. They advocate the adoption of strategic management accounting which seeks both to evaluate the benefits which 'sales yield over a long-term horizon', and 'to estimate the enterprise costs relative to its competitors'. This 'can be used to allow investment appraisal to incorporate strategic characteristics'.

Management accounting practice has not ignored the problems of the traditional methods found in many texts, but has already been pursuing approaches which have an external perspective over a long time horizon. This article presents a particular example of a company utilising the philosophy of strategic management accounting, in response to its own business needs.

Stapylton is a case study which concerns a company's response to action by a major competitor considered to pose a threat to the company's market position. The case considers the manner in which management accounting information was gathered both from within the organisation and from external sources.

By contrast with the concentration of management accounting literature on the use of information already collected by existing internal systems, it illustrates the process by which special-purpose data was actually generated to meet strategic needs. Management accounting carried out its function by capturing and stimulating the creation of new information by the company, obtained by searching the environment outside that under the direct control of the organisation as well as from internal sources.

9.3 Case details

Quote: 'I can't stand apportionments: they generate a lot of heat and not much light.'

This remark was made by the company management accountant and is the key to the philosophy underlying the way the internal accounting system is structured and used. Apportionments do have to be made for certain purposes, but these are not normally ones which also play a part in decision-making.

The management accounting system operated by Stapylton contrasts strongly with traditional management accounts. The latter are frequently no more than actual compared with budgeted results, the figures mostly being compiled on an absorption basis (a basis whose origins may well have been forgotten).

Company structure

A matrix scheme has been adopted. The 'Operating Company' is the organisation as a whole. It is broken down into business centres, which are each composed of several product lines. For each product line within a business centre there is a management team comprising members with expertise in production, marketing, sales and finance, each with a link to their respective functional heads at the company level as well as having direct responsibility for the business centre and its product lines. Product lines, business centres and the Stapylton company as a whole are all considered to be responsibility centres within a hierarchical structure that extends upwards to major operational divisions within the Group. However, the functional relationships do not extend to the Group.

Appointments are actually made to functional departments, but the principal allegiance of staff was seen to be to the product line.

Planning

A rolling annual budget planning cycle is in operation. Budgets are established for a period of five years ahead, with the first year being the detailed budget for the current operating period. Taking 1989 as the starting point, for example, there would be a firm operating budget for 1989 to be used as the basis for control; a more tentative plan for 1990, which in turn would be drawn up as a firm programme for 1990 around September 1989, and beyond that exist three further outline annual plans up to 1993.

A new present value evaluation of each five-year period is carried out, with a comparison made of each succeeding plan against previous ones.

The process of adopting a rolling budget basis for periods within the current year ahead is not yet implemented, but is under development.

This planning cycle is supported by a process which continually monitors the changing competitive position of the company as well as the effect of proposed internal policy changes and known/expected changes in current business revenues and costs. A major feature of the plan is the explicit statement of the environmental assumptions under which it is made. This would include specific reference to significant threats or potential opportunities which might arise given certain changes. Clearly, this aids the monitoring of the competitive situation, which is part of the on-going activity of management accounting within the operating division.

Management accounts report

The general layout of the report is illustrated below in Figure 1.

Figure 1: Management accounts

Company summary report

	Operating company	*Business centre*	*Individual product lines*
Sales	x	x	x
Prime costs	x	x	x
Gross margin	x	x	x
Direct marketing	x	x	x
Net product margin	x	x	x
Product attributable indirect costs	x	x	x
Product contribution	x	x	x
Business attributable indirect costs	x	x	
Business centre contribution	x	x	
Factory general overheads			
Selling expenses	x		
Company administration			
Company marketing			
Operating company contribution	x		
Apportioned services	x		
Gross trading profit	x		

x = entries made.

The basic costing distinction which is drawn is between direct and indirect expenses, with the indirect element being analysed according to the degree to which a given item is attributable (if at all) to product lines and business centres.

Costs are broadly analysed as follows:

Direct costs

- raw material } prime costs
- packaging } prime costs
- direct labour } prime costs
- direct marketing
- inflation assessment/adjustment

This analysis is carried out across the matrix of the management accounts and leads to the definition of both a gross and net product margin.

Directly attributable overhead (indirect costs) to products and business centres

Products are segregated into major product types forming a business centre, and directly attributable overheads are defined in relation to both products themselves and to the operation of the production departments through which they pass.

Product contributions and a business centre contribution are derived.

Indirect costs attributable to the operating company

Factory general overhead, selling expenses, company administration and company marketing costs which cannot be directly attributed to products or business centres are not apportioned to either. They appear on the management accounts solely as the responsibility of the operating company management. Their deduction from the aggregated business centre contribution gives the operating company contribution.

Apportioned services charges

These are part of shared services costs at the operating company level. They are apportionments from the central controlling company, but innovative in that the apportionment is made up of a part fixed, part variable charge. The variable element is based on what the company would have had to pay for the service had it been supplied from outside. The fixed cost is a relatively small residual element.

Planning targets

The operating company has a required return target on assets of 22½ per cent before interest and tax. This figure is also used as the minimum discounted requirement for evaluation of capital expenditures as well as the five-year business programme.

Cash flow is stated to be of prime interest, particularly in the long term, though it should be noted that the business level 'contribution' stated in the above management accounts is after deduction of depreciation.

In order to obtain a single cash flow figure for the business, this earlier deduction of depreciation is compensated for by defining cash flow as the business centre contribution plus any decrease in operating assets or minus any increase in them, within a given period.

However, it is still not strictly a pure cash flow because accounting is on an accruals basis. A more accurate description of the figure may be 'working funds flow', since the contribution figure contains elements of an accruals-based profit figure. The quantitative effect of not adopting a strict cash flow definition may be small but represents a technical feature adopted to meet the practical demands made upon the accounting system.

Traditional total standard cost records are also maintained, despite their obvious differences with the cost basis of the current management accounts. They are required to produce full-cost stock valuations for statutory accounts purposes. Full standard product cost is based on prime cost as defined earlier. To this figure is added a figure for general overhead recovery derived from a standard recovery rate based on volume.

Normal variances are obtained at the prime cost stage, and a procedure for reconciliation of the full standard costs with the management accounts exists. A book-keeping scheme for handling such a reconciliation is illustrated in Appendix A.

Features of the Stapylton management accounting system

The company pays considerable attention to the way costs may be attributed to the well-defined accounting units. Costs which may be expected to vary with volume of activity, and/or be under the direct control of management at the various defined stages of the business, are clearly distinguished in each case.

The emphasis, it should be noted, is on the way costs may be attributed to products/business segments, rather than purely on variability with volume. The latter concept, however, is employed in particular situations (see the later section: Directly attributable overhead).

Direct labour

Although direct labour is part of prime products costs, which might make it appear classifiable as variable expense, it is recognised that there is a hard core of the direct labour force which is a fixed cost in the immediate future and probably in the medium term of one to two years ahead. This situation may not be dissimilar to that facing many companies.

However, from a cost behaviour point of view, the company is fortunate to be able to expand or contract direct labour availability within limits to match volume changes in the very short term.

The factory is sited in an area where it is traditional working practice that very short-term contracts (one week) may be used at times as required, to meet increasing demand. It is a practice accepted by both unions and workers.

As far as the company is concerned, the short-term contract policy is naturally adopted in preference to having a large permanent workforce, with the prospect of having to use temporary lay-offs at 80 per cent pay from time to time. It is a practice which may also help avoid the otherwise occasional need to put on a second or evening shift.

The nature of these direct labour costs is of significance when considering views on the management accounting treatment of the behaviour of costs. In this case, all prime costs can be varied in response to volume changes in the short term down to the level of a week. As a result, output plans can be closely matched with labour requirements and the short-term selected labour capacity can be utilised, given that any excess of actual output over that demanded will only result in a short-term inventory stock level fluctuation. Prime costs may be seen as marginal costs which vary in both a dependent and smooth, rather than step-like, manner in response to volume change within a relevant range of 20 per cent of normal activity.

Directly attributable overhead

Since it is identified at various levels, this category of expense is not so precisely defined. The central concept used to distinguish these costs is that they must be 'managed' to be in line with the level of business generated. As such there is no automatic or dependent response in cost levels to changes in volume of activity.

By contrast with the prime costs described above, the level of cost in this category is set by decisions preceding the actual activity and intended to provide the necessary capacity to meet the needs of the volume of activity which ensues. The costs incurred are variable primarily to the extent that management decides to vary the resources to be provided, and it is in this sense that they are 'managed'.

Deviation in cost levels, in the time period subsequent to the managerial preselection of the level of costs, may arise as a result of changes in the efficiency of the use and acquisition of resources. However, these are of relatively small significance in most cases, the notable exception occurring when the activity is actually so much in excess of that anticipated that it is necessary to supplement the original planned provision of resources by using resources more expensive, less suitable or in a less efficient manner than usual. This exception is of such impact that efforts are made to ensure it is almost always avoided.

In considering the implementation of this concept of 'managed' cost, attributable costs are those within the ability of the responsible management team to control. At the lower level they will consist of payments for the utilities such as power, indirect labour and supervision. They also include depreciation, where the ability to vary is obviously largely non-existent except over a relatively long period – and then only if managers have authority over acquisitions and disposals.

In general, no specific time horizon is quoted over which results must be achieved, but year-end results are certainly an important stage at which progress is examined. Additionally, regular monitoring also takes place at the end of each monthly accounting period.

Directly attributable costs represent approximately 58 per cent of total cost at the level of the operating company and hence a clearly significant segment of cost which is regarded as controllable. Administration and selling expenses are regarded as expenses of the company rather than product groups, though they are analysed in a similar manner to the attributable overhead to identify the 'manageable' element.

Variable overheads are not distinguished as such in the management accounts. However, the management have made use of the concept in relation to special decisions. In these cases they attempted to subdivide attributable overhead expense to specifically identify those costs which would change with the selection of the alternatives. As a result, *ad hoc* exercises were required to meet the needs of significant decisions as they arose.

No formal statistical analysis of cost is considered necessary by the company, since so few expenses of any significance are viewed as susceptible to traditional methods of statistical cost estimation, managerial action being thought of as the critical factor in determining the level of cost actually incurred.

9.4 Concluding remarks

The system described above has been in operation for only a few years. The present management accountant took over his duties in the company in 1984, with a system which was very centralised, causing the unit to be more of a budget centre than a business. The change to the latter system has been accomplished in a relatively short period of time. It has been accompanied by a restructuring of the accounts in order to provide the business with information which is seen as being intrinsically a part of the overall information needed to guide its activities, make decisions, and measure performance, rather than being a (neglected) piece of routine data which is not actually useful.

The way in which information is collected and analysed minimises the extent to which arbitrary apportionment is carried out. Full cost reporting for budget planning and control purposes is regarded as a 'waste of time'. At the same time, a pragmatic view of cost behaviour is taken which does not rely upon a clear-cut classification of costs (which may be spurious as to relationships with other factors and are oversimplified) in order to lend itself to analytical and statistically based examination.

Very few cost items can be claimed to be purely variable with volume in the immediate sense of adjusting in a continuous and direct way to changes in volume of output. Even in the present company, their limited category of prime costs does not wholly match this view of variability.

This leaves the question of how costs behave very much dependent on what is under consideration – general changes in the level of business, new products, new technology and so on. The way costs will move and respond to these changes will depend greatly on the pressure applied by management in each individual case – hence the general conclusion that costs should be viewed as being 'managed', rather than behaving in some automatic and predictable way.

References

Bromwich, M and Bhimani, A (1989), *Management Accounting: Evolution not Revolution*, CIMA. (This book now has a successor in *Management Accounting: Pathways to Progress* (1994).
Cooper, R (1989), 'You need a new cost system when...', *Harvard Business Review*, Jan./Feb.
Cooper, R and Kaplan, R S (1987), 'How cost accounting systematically distorts product costs', in Bruns, W J and Kaplan, R S (eds), *Accounting and Management: Field Study Perspectives*, Harvard Business School Press.
Johnson, H T and Kaplan, R S (1987), *Relevance Lost: The Rise and Fall of Management Accounting*, Harvard Business School Press.

9.5 *Appendix*

Procedure for reconciling full standard costs with direct cost for stock valuation

For example: assume there is a 200 per cent recovery rate of overhead based on direct costs of £1000 in a particular period when output was 100 units. The entries to record cost incurred would be:

Debit	Stock	£3,000	
Credit	Wages		£1,000
Credit	Other suspense		£2,000

Subsequent sales of stock having a direct cost content of £80 for £350 would be recorded as:

Credit	Sales		£3,500
Debit	Debtors	£3,500	
Debit	Cost of sales	£800	
Debit	Overhead suspense	£1,600	
Credit	Stock		£2,400

If overheads incurred actually amount to £1800 this would be recorded as:

Debit	Overhead expense	£1,800	
Credit	Overhead creditor		£1,800

At the year end, adjustments are made to allow for the overhead spending variance so that reported stock figures include overhead at actual rather than standard rates. In this case the stock figure should include one-fifth of the overheads incurred. This proportion is represented by the twenty units in stock out of the 100 produced. As a result, the overhead suspense account requires adjusting to one-fifth of £1800, i.e. £360. This adjustment is implemented as:

Debit	Overhead suspense	£40	
Credit	Stock		£40

In the management accounts the overhead suspense account is treated as a reduction in stock values, while added back to profit for financial accounting purposes.

Profit & loss account	*Management accounts* £	*Financial accounts* £
Sales	3,500	
Cost of sales	800	
Contribution	2,700	
Overhead incurred	1,800	
Profit	900	900
Add back overhead suspense		360
Reported profit		1,260

Changes in Balance Sheet

Increase in debits	Mgmt accounts		Financial accounts	*Increase in credits*	Mgmt accounts	Financial accounts
	£	£	£		£	£
Stock	560		560	Creditors o'head	1,800	1,800
Less overhead suspense	360	200		Direct costs	1,000	1,000
					2,800	2,800
Debtors		3,500	3,500	P & L	900	1,260
		3,700	4,060		3,700	4,060

The adjustments of overhead to actual cost levels is carried out only for the purpose of year-end accounts. At the start of the subsequent years it is necessary to carry out further adjustment, this time to ensure that the opening account is amended so that the overhead suspense account is consistent with the standard overhead rates for that subsequent year. Again adjustment is carried out by double entry in the overhead suspense and stock accounts.

9.6 *Questions*

1. Do you consider the reported comment of Stapylton's accountant (quoted in the Case background) with respect to absorption costing to be justified? In all circumstances?

2. How might you account for the fact that absorption costing is still the predominant costing system in UK industry today?

3. Compare and contrast textbook approaches to the questions of cost behaviour and cost control with that of Stapylton. What explanations could be given to any differences which are noted?

4. To what extent do you consider that the company's analysis of costs and activities is being carried out along activity based costing (ABC) lines?

6. In the event of a major decision such as a product line being recommended for closure, to what extent would the new management accounting information system be able to provide all the necessary information?

7. Irrespective of your answer to 6, what difficulties would be experienced in such a situation were an absorption costing system in operation?

8. Does the new system also render standard costing and standard cost variance analysis unnecessary?

10 Stapylton B

10.1 Synopsis

Stapylton is a case study which concerns a company's response to action taken by a major competitor considered to pose a threat to the company's market position. The case considers the manner in which management accounting information was gathered both from within the organisation and from external sources.

By contrast with the concentration of management accounting literature on the use of information already collected by existing internal systems, it illustrates the process by which special-purpose data was actually generated to meet strategic needs. Management accounting carried out its function by capturing and stimulating the creation of new information; this was obtained by searching the environment outside the organisation as well as from internal sources.

10.2 Background

The company and its product market

Throughout the period under consideration, the company, Stapylton Ltd, operates as a wholly owned subsidiary of a very large international group with over 30,000 employees and worldwide sales in excess of £1 billion. Stapylton's products, which are described as in the hygiene and cleaning materials industry, are sold direct to retail outlets, principally the supermarket chains. Within the Group the company concentrates on a small range of closely related products of a basic rather than luxury nature, which it sells through its own sales force. Although brand names are considered of some importance, emphasis has always been placed on a Company, rather than Group, identity for this range of products.

Stapylton has a multifunction management team which has considerable managerial autonomy extending to pricing, marketing, accounting and production policies within limits prescribed initially by budgets expressed in 'cash flow' terms. Cash flow for these purposes can be interpreted as working capital funds flow, sales revenue and expenditures being recognised at the date of invoice rather than the actual receipt or payment of cash.

Although Stapylton had been a member of the Group for many years, substantial reorganisation within the Group led to a significant change in the management structure within Stapylton from the start of the 1984/5 financial year. It was at this time that the company was granted its autonomy in marketing and price volume policies. Previously, the Group Board had been responsible for determining output quantities based on Group marketing policies, and Stapylton was assessed by its performance against standard product costs.

From September 1984, Stapylton was responsible for the design of its own management accounting systems and internal structure. New systems had been introduced and there was further delegation, when responsibility for each of six business centres representing a cluster of closely related product lines within Stapylton was assigned to a team. Each team included sales, marketing, finance, procurement and production executives.

Corporate performance, and executive rewards for Stapylton as a whole, were assessed largely on the basis of revenue net of traceable costs expressed as a ratio of operating assets. However, this was subject to meeting the cash or funds flow requirements of the budget. The required minimum return represented by this ratio was set at 22½ per cent. It is of particular interest that this figure was also used as the discount rate for evaluation of both capital expenditures, and a five-year business programme to be submitted to Group management. The company occupied a clearly distinguishable site in central Lancashire which provided a basis for the tracing of costs and of assets to the company.

The manner in which the management accounting function acts is considered in this article in relation to a particular product type representing over a quarter of the company's annual value added. The market for this particular product comprises branded and own label sectors. Only five brand names are of any significance in the branded sector, the dominant share coming from just two brands, those owned by Stapylton and Lynnfields. In addition, supermarket chains used all the major UK and some foreign manufacturers to produce competing products using the various chains' own label; such chains' own label products represented more than half the total UK market sales, having shown increases in market share of some 10 per cent since 1984.

During this same period, Lynnfields had seen its share of the total market decrease from 17 per cent down to almost 12 per cent, while Stapylton had achieved a small increase from 1984 when it had a share roughly equal to Lynnfields. Stapylton's competitive success was achieved while maintaining a premium of about 5 per cent in the selling price.

Marketing information

The interest shown by the management accounting function in the external environment is partly revealed by that function's detailed awareness of the price premium. Monthly reports prepared by a national market research agency which quantified a number of aspects of consumer activity in this particular product market were received by the management accounting function. It was their responsibility to distribute information contained in these reports to other functions. Major emphasis was given to information on market share and the prices paid by consumers for their purchases.

This information was supplemented by the company's own weekly survey. Data was collected by sales staff making observations at retail outlets and collated with competitors' and retailers' advertising material gleaned from the media by the accounting function. The fact that these duties were undertaken by accounting personnel may be taken as an indicator both of the range of activities considered the domain of the accounting function, and of the integrated nature of the management team responsible for the product type.

The price–volume information was considered at the regular monthly meetings of the management team. Although there had been no attempt to carry out formal analysis of the data, there was general recognition that volume, and in particular market share, showed a sensitivity to the relative product price represented by the size of the premium.

Two factors are considered by the company to be of special significance in supporting the maintenance of this premium. The first is a feature of the product itself. The particular process adopted in its production results in a product which, while not changing the nature or performance of the product, makes it easier to use. Although this may endow a degree of superiority, market information had revealed that small increases in price resulted in sufficient shifting of consumption away from the product to suggest that this would provide only limited brand loyalty.

The second significant feature to which the price premium was attributed arises from the package size. The origins of this are historic. At the time of metrication, whilst the 'own label' products and that of major competitors had moved to a 500 ml. package, Stapylton used a 400 ml. container of distinctive shape and colour. This size difference meant that despite the 5 per cent premium, the unit shelf price *per container* of the Stapylton product was some 16 per cent lower than that of its competitor, Lynnfields, and some 10 per cent below the own label shelf price.

Stapylton considered that, despite any qualitative advantage its product possessed, the obscuring of direct comparison between unit prices by the use of a different package size had played a part in maintaining the premium during a period of growth in their share of the branded market. It was also suggested that the package size emphasised the quality difference at the time of purchase; Lynnfields' product was less obviously different from the own label products and it was against these that Lynnfields had been losing sales volume.

10.3 Case details

Towards the end of January 1984, Stapylton heard that Lynnfields was planning to modify its own facilities to begin using 400 ml. packs. Lynnfields' move was identified through Stapylton's own marketing function. One of the smaller retail chains, operating almost exclusively in Scotland, had been threatening to discontinue stocking Lynnfields' product. In defence of this customer relationship, Lynnfields had been prepared to release information about its repackaging which would reveal its product's lower selling price per ml. This retailer put pressure on Stapylton by asking their Scottish sales office for price reductions in the face of Lynnfields' change. The request was transmitted to Stapylton 's Lancashire head office the same day.

Identifying responses

At the first meeting of Stapylton's management team a number of short-term decisions were taken. It was recognised that the increased visibility of the price differential was likely to have a significant effect on turnover unless some reaction was made. The competitive initiative of Lynnfields was not entirely unexpected, so when it was identified there was immediate awareness of the need to respond. Little had been done to identify the strategy to adopt in response in the longer term. 'We had not thought out what our specific response would be if this did happen, but then we would have to have made guesses as to how they would do it and when. There were still so many unknowns that we considered it was preferable not to work out our total response.' However, it was immediately agreed that for the month of February a special 5 per cent discount would be offered. This effectively removed the premium and the objective was to offer this as a form of short-term promotion rather than being seen as a response to the particular competitive action.

At this initial meeting estimates of the likely effects suggested that a fall in turnover of up to 20 per cent could be anticipated. The resultant potential drop in profit was of such proportion that the Stapylton management team considered it appropriate to notify Group Management and to involve them in the final selection of any decision to be made.

Stapylton's management team defined its own role as the identification and analysis of options and recommendation of a preferred option to the Group Board. It was considered that some of the options would have significant implications over a period of up to five years and that decisions affecting such a long term should be referred to the Group Board. Some comments by Stapylton's management confirm this: 'We would expect to make decisions of this type ourselves but here it was going to have corporate implications. . . . We saw our role as identifying the options and then recommending because we could not assume their [the Group's] objectives were short term or long term.' This statement reflects the significance which the Stapylton management attributed to this decision and their recognition that this could have a potential impact on other operations within the Group due to the effects on Group cash flow.

The major concern was that this competitive action could lead to a failure by Stapylton to meet their original profit forecast. In line with the rest of the group, their financial year ran to 30 September so this change was likely to have an impact on at least a half-year's results. The immediate task of countering the threat by discounting prices needed to be replaced by one of minimising the longer-term impact. Cost reduction was considered but it was decided immediately that, although there may be some opportunities for cost savings, the additional cost involved in maintaining Stapylton's difference in product quality resulted in a valuable advantage which should not be given up.

Other options were for a substantial price reduction or for an advertising policy designed to reinforce and emphasise the quality differences of Stapylton's own product. The relationship between cost savings, price reductions and advertising were not worked out at this stage and it became the role of the management accounting function to co-ordinate the quantitative analysis of these options.

In addition to its co-ordinating role, management accounting made a significant contribution to the assessment of Lynnfields' specific policies. This activity made considerable use of the ability of the accounting function to collect information from the external environment. The role of co-ordinator placed the management accountant in a unique and powerful position which he used in his task of capturing non-routine information and in the related activity of managing the implementation of the chosen option.

Data collection

Stapylton management identified three areas of data need:

- First, information was required to establish the effects on Stapylton's cost of any resulting changes in volume or of efficiency through modifying production methods or facilities;
- Second, it was necessary to assess the potential competitive reaction by Lynnfields in response to a policy change by Stapylton;
- Third, information was needed in quantified form to assess the effects of price and advertising policies on Stapylton.

Cost information

The structure of the system of regular cost collection operated by Stapylton had been introduced in September 1981. For each product type standards are available for prime costs, which may be considered variable, and these standards are updated quarterly for known and predicted price changes to represent the anticipated costs for the quarter to which they will be applied.

This product type is treated as a business centre, management reports highlighting the excess of sales revenue over the sum of prime costs at actual levels and those overhead costs which can be directly attributed to the product type. No attempts are made for these purposes to apportion to the product group or company costs which are not wholly traceable. Further, there is no regular separation of the fixed and variable elements of overhead costs which can be traced to the product group or company.

The management decided that special-purpose data was needed. There was an on-going internal major review of efficiency and this was sharpened up. The company had to face immediately policy decisions which needed to be considered within a longer-term horizon. Significantly, these decisions would be affected by the anticipated changes both in cost level and in the cost structure. In turn, the selection of plant capacity levels would both change the cost structure and be dependent upon the policy to be adopted. Further, there was the need for more urgent attention to changes, in the light of the present threat which was expected to reduce revenues and/or put up marketing costs.

The needs for information were met largely by speeding up the on-going efficiency review and by detailed consideration of the elements of directly attributable overhead. Discussion with appropriate operating and functional personnel aided the identification of what changes in overhead spending could be anticipated at different levels of operations.

It was of key importance that, at this stage, the management accounting staff were to use cost information produced on a different basis to that regularly reported; the latter had become familiar to sales, marketing and production management because of its regular use.

Assessment of the competitor

At this stage, the full details of the changes the competitor was going to make were not known. The management team set themselves a target of finalising their response by the end of February with the intention of being able to provide a firm statement to retailers at about the time it expected Lynnfields to make its action widely known. In order to assess its own response, Stapylton wanted to establish in as much detail as possible the Lynnfields' action and to consider what subsequent competitive responses Lynnfields might make when Stapylton's own plans became public.

'Once we started looking at the effect it had on us, we started to look at the effect on them from our response.'

The first requirement was to establish the competitors' costs, both regular on-going production costs as well as the costs of implementing this particular decision. This was used as one basis for establishing their pricing policy following their change in packaging. In addition, this could be used to assess Lynnfields' perception of the market changes they anticipated and their scope and incentive to pursue further competitive activity.

A number of sources of information are available to quantify and attribute financial values to the activities of competitors. Like other companies that have been observed, Stapylton analysed their competitors' performance regularly and already had in operation active mechanisms intended to collect the available relevant information.

In addition to the observation of selling prices and the purchase of market research, Stapylton already made use of public information contained in the press, in broker reports, from common suppliers of both equipment and raw chemicals, and in financial reports. This information was used in a routine way in the regular meetings of management in which consideration of competitors was as much a recurrent agenda item as consideration of the customer retail outlets. The marketing management were not the only members of the product team keen 'to know our competitor cost profile as well as his market stance'.

The additional efforts made by Stapylton to measure its competitors' costs can be considered. Stapylton also made a product using the standard process adopted by Lynnfields and most of the rest of the industry in manufacturing for the 'own-label' product of a major retail chain. Stapylton's understanding of the methods of production adopted by Lynnfields had emerged both from negotiations with retail chains concerning own-label production and from discussions with process machine manufacturers. Enquiries concerning the production activities by such manufacturers indicated that Lynnfields did not plan to modify the quality of their product to incorporate the special processing that distinguished the Stapylton product. This was also consistent with the literature made available to the retailer in Scotland. As a result, an estimate of Lynnfields' prime costs could be made which, although not based on actual information about the operations, was considered sufficiently accurate as a starting point.

The cost structure identified by this process of simulating the activities of the competitor was checked in the first instance by an analysis of Lynnfields' company accounts. In this case, Lynnfields, which was part of a small group of companies, was a separate legal entity whose product range was dominated by the product of interest. Indications of modifications in Lynnfields' operations were identified in the Directors' reports which outlined capital investment plans and labour changes.

The next major information source was provided by investment analysis undertaken by stock-brokers who had been looking at the industry. This type of analysis contains confirmation of existing practices but extends to providing informed estimates of forecast company activity, volume, capital investment plans and profit intentions.

Additional data was also produced which attempted to establish the cost of the change in policy in the Lynnfields company, taking into account operating costs associated with the new package size and Lynnfields own advertising costs. These advertising costs were established using two sources: first, Lynnfields' own indications given to its retail customers to show the extent of its new sales drive on the consumer market; second, information given by advertising agencies to Stapylton to encourage similar expenditure by Stapylton to match Lynnfields' efforts. It was considered that these sources were likely to produce estimates on the high side and suitable reduction was made by utilising the experience of the degree of overestimate included in similar information on other products in the past. Putting all the data together a number of computations were performed in order to clarify Stapylton's understanding of its competitor's future actions.

With estimates of prime costs and other variable costs, its rival's contribution to fixed costs could be established at different forecast selling prices. The volume of sales required at each contribution level in order first to meet the forecasts published by brokers, second to make the capital costs of the policy change worthwhile and finally to justify the total capital investment proposal were mapped out and assessed for feasibility. These price options were explored to attempt to predict the new Lynnfields selling price and then to establish Lynnfields' subsequent scope for further response. The information produced was discussed by the full management team at company level and was considered vital to formulating a response.

Two potential forms of competitive action were identified: direct general price competition in the consumer market; an expansion of volume discounts and discounts offered to retail outlets to enable greater margins to be obtained by the retailer.

Price and advertising information

The final major area of data collection was the assessment of the implications of Staplyton's own marketing policy. The objective was to give specific consideration to a repricing policy and/or an extended advertising policy. This is a topic which was considered by the management accountant to pose particular problems in producing useful data. He was proud of the technique he developed.

'My problem, as the accountant, was to pin down the marketing man to having to quantify the various options. Accounting played the right part and made them quantify. I would ask, "If you want £1m for advertising what will you give me in increased sales volume? What would be the effect of a price cut of 2 per cent, 4 per cent, zero?" These questions I made them answer so it was capable of quantification, but it was up to me to work them out.'

It was made clear in his discussions with marketing that the information obtained would not only be used directly in the formulation of a response to the particular situation they faced at this time, but would also be incorporated in budget requirements. The management accountants considered that their ability to elicit information from marketing executives was significantly aided by the process adopted. The accountants were able to use their monopoly position. Only they had access to all the relevant data and they selected the policy for cost determination which resulted in the valuation of the benefits of alternative possible outcomes.

The management accountant's own statement emphasises the relative positions he and his marketing colleague held in relation to the establishment of relevant data and its managerial implications. Information was not freely available but had to be obtained from those who possessed or were able to formulate it, possibly without their willing co-operation. He 'made them quantify'.

A further task was to ensure that the information revealed in this way provided a valid basis on which to make the comparisons. Using the data as the basis both for budget setting and for providing resources provided disincentives to distort information in either direction. He could 'pin down' his marketing colleagues, making them concerned with the quality of the information they provided.

He was able to make marketing quantify the options by maintaining his monopoly position of knowledge of forecast outcomes: 'it was up to me to work them out'.

Although the marketing function envisaged that the situation might provide them with additional funding, they were made aware that this would only be provided if net benefits to the organisation would be produced. They had to trade off additional funding against higher performance requirements. However, they were unable to calculate for themselves the minimum improvement in performance needed to justify a given level of additional funding.

Having been placed in this dilemma it was in the interest of the marketing function to provide realistic data. The management accountants produced statements of alternative possible results to permit comparison to be made between the various combinations suggested and agreed to by the marketing function. This identified the chosen strategy in terms of sales volume, price and media expenditure.

The process of focusing on suitable alternative strategies was achieved through interaction within the management team over a period of about three weeks in February 1987. Several attempts were made at setting out comparisons during that time, and the example shown below represents a tabulation utilised at a meeting held in the week immediately prior to submission to the Group Board; earlier versions adopted the same form of presentation. The tables shown present four major options which consider alternative policies of pricing and media expenditure.

Utilisation of data

The analysis illustrated by Tables 1–4 was used to justify the recommendation and selection of the policy represented by Table 3, primarily on the basis of the size of the NPV based on the 22½ per cent discount rate set by the Group. Table 1 shows the anticipated results over five years under the assumption that no additional expenditure is made on media advertising. It incorporates the effects of an immediate loss of most of the price premium reflected by reduction in selling price of some 4 per cent combined with a simultaneous drop in volume of 15 per cent from the prevailing level of 1.18 million units per annum to 1.0 million units per annum (where each unit represents a tray of two dozen containers).

The effects of a substantial and sustained programme of media advertising are presented in Table 2. This is designed to show what would be necessary to maintain prevailing levels of price and volume.

Table 3 examines the results of adopting a strategy which concentrates on responding specifically to the competitive threat. This comprises more modest media expenditure over a limited period coupled with a policy of cutting the price premium in order to protect sales volumes. In carrying out these projections a number of combinations of price and volume policies were considered and the consequences of changing price by 1 per cent steps computed. By way of illustration Table 4 shows the results expected if the pricing policy had been to maintain the premium during the period of the more modest media campaign itself, taking account of the volume reductions that would result, and of the effects subsequent to the period of advertising.

As indicated earlier, the unit cost included in the calculations was produced specially for this exercise making allowance for the cost savings resulting from the efficiency reviews. This was an attempt to identify only those costs which would be changed by volume fluctuations within the ranges considered. All apportionments of overheads not directly traceable to this product type were excluded as not fitting the 'managed cost' category described earlier. No specific adjustments were made for inflation, all calculations being made using current prices and costs.

Table 1

No media campaign

	Year 0	*Year 1*	*Year 2*	*Year 3*	*Year 4*	*Year 5*
Sales quantity	1,180	1,000	1,000	1,000	1,000	1,000
	£	£	£	£	£	£
Price/unit	10.2	9.8	9.8	9.8	9.8	9.8
Revenue	12,036	9,800	9,800	9,800	9,800	9,800
Unit cost	6.3	6.3	6.3	6.3	6.3	6.3
Attributable cost	7,434	6,300	6,300	6,300	6,300	6,300
Contribution	4,602	3,500	3,500	3,500	3,500	3,500
Media expenditure	0	0	0	0	0	
Working capital	–1,050	0	0	0	0	1,050
Annual cash flow	3,552	3,500	3,500	3,500	3,500	4,550
NPV						13,849.15
Discount rate		0.225				

Table 2

High media campaign

	Year 0	*Year 1*	*Year 2*	*Year 3*	*Year 4*	*Year 5*
Sales quantity	1,180	1,180	1,180	1,180	1,180	1,180
	£	£	£	£	£	£
Price/unit	10.2	10.2	10.2	10.2	10.2	10.2
Revenue	12,036	12,036	12,036	12,036	12,036	12,036
Unit cost	6.3	6.3	6.3	6.3	6.3	6.3
Attributable cost	7,434	7,434	7,434	7,434	7,434	7,434
Contribution	4,602	4,602	4,602	4,602	4,602	4,602
Media expenditure	0	1,000	1,000	1,000	1,000	1,000
Working capital	–1,239	0	0	0	0	1,239
Annual cash flow	3,363	3,602	3,602	3,602	3,602	4,841
NPV						14,017.66
Discount rate		0.225				

Table 3

Low media (premium foregone)

	Year 0	*Year 1*	*Year 2*	*Year 3*	*Year 4*	*Year 5*
Sales quantity	1,180	1,180	1,180	1,120	1,060	1,000
	£	£	£	£	£	£
Price/unit	10.2	9.8	9.8	9.8	9.8	9.8
Revenue	12,036	11,564	11,564	10,976	10,388	9,800
Unit cost	6.3	6.3	6.3	6.3	6.3	6.3
Attributable cost	7,434	7,434	7,434	7,056	6,678	6,300
Contribution	4,602	4,130	4,130	3,920	3,710	3,500
Media expenditure	0	700	500	0	0	0
Working capital	–1,239	0	–63	–63	–63	1,050
Annual cash flow	3,363	3,430	3,693	3,983	3,773	4,550
NPV						14,115.60
Discount rate		0.225				

Table 4

Low media (volume reduced)

	Year 0	*Year 1*	*Year 2*	*Year 3*	*Year 4*	*Year 5*
Sales quantity	1,180	1,000	1,000	1,000	1,000	1,000
	£	£	£	£	£	£
Price/unit	10.2	10.2	10.2	10.07	9.94	9.8
Revenue	12,036	10,200	10,200	10,070	9,940	9,800
Unit cost	6.3	6.3	6.3	6.3	6.3	6.3
Attributable cost	7,434	6,300	6,300	6,300	6,300	6,300
Contribution	4,602	3,900	3,900	3,700	3,640	3,500
Media expenditure	0	700	500	0	0	0
Working capital	–1,050	0	0	0	0	1,050
Annual cash flow	3,552	3,200	3,400	3,770	3,640	4,550
NPV						13,746.66
Discount rate		0.225				

For these purposes depreciation was specifically excluded and an allowance was made for working capital changes so that the annual outcomes could be treated as cash flow.

In addition to their use in justifying the selection of a particular policy, the analysis shown in the above tables duly formed the basis for the product group's budget.

In particular, the marketing function accepted the pricing policy and reduction in premium reflected by Table 3.

Sensitivity of results

As indicated in the previous section, the accountants collected information to produce a sensitivity analysis considering £0.10 changes in price by getting the product group marketing staff to supply data combinations of price and volume under each policy. Consider, as an example, the policy of high expenditure on media advertising as presented in Table 2. The specific price of 10.2 combined with high media expenditure gave constant volumes of 1.18 million units and an NPV of £14.018 million. The full analysis of high media price policies reveals the following:

Price (£/unit)	9.8	9.9	10.0	10.1	10.2	10.3	10.4
Volume (000's)	1,235	1,230	1,220	1,205	1,180	1,145	1,105
NPV (£'000)	13,189	13,491	13,742	13,936	14,018	13,979	13,865

In this case of high media expenditure, the price of £10.20 was selected because the predicted volume of 1.18 million units associated with that price would result in the highest expected net present value of £14,018,000.

The price–volume combinations supplied by the marketing function were not explored further, no attempt being made to see how sensitive the choice of price might be to small changes in volume. Whilst such examination could be carried out with some ease using standard spreadsheet procedures available for use on personal computers, the company did not use spreadsheet software for this exercise. The view taken that the agreed price–volume combinations were not open to further investigation was consistent with the treatment of the data as the future marketing budget. This process was used to fix the budget for marketing in terms of volume, price and media expenditure for the five-year planning horizon subject to change only on the basis of a full reappraisal.

Figure 1 is presented here to aid interpretation of this view. The figure shows a graph of the price–volume combinations supplied by the marketing staff (AB) set alongside that of those combinations which would have yielded the same net present value (£14,018,000) as the chosen combination (CD). This chosen combination of £10.20 and £1,180,000 units is shown as point E and, of course, AB and CD are tangential at this point. It can be seen that at a price of £10.3, annual volumes of more than 1,149,000 would have made this a preferable combination to that chosen. This represents a change of little over 0.25 per cent from that offered of 1,145,000.

Although one must recognise the reluctance to enter further dialogue with marketing staff because this might undermine the value of the data for budgeting, the choice of combination was also dependent upon other input values, in particular the level of attributable cost per unit. Using this high media case as an example again, it is possible to show that at unit cost levels of £6.68 or above, the combination of 1,145,000 units and £10.30 per unit produces superior net present values to the chosen combination. Similarly at levels of cost per unit below £5.19 the combination of a £10.10 selling price and 1,205,000 units becomes superior to that chosen.

Figure 1 Graph of price–volume combinations (high media – constant NPV curve added)

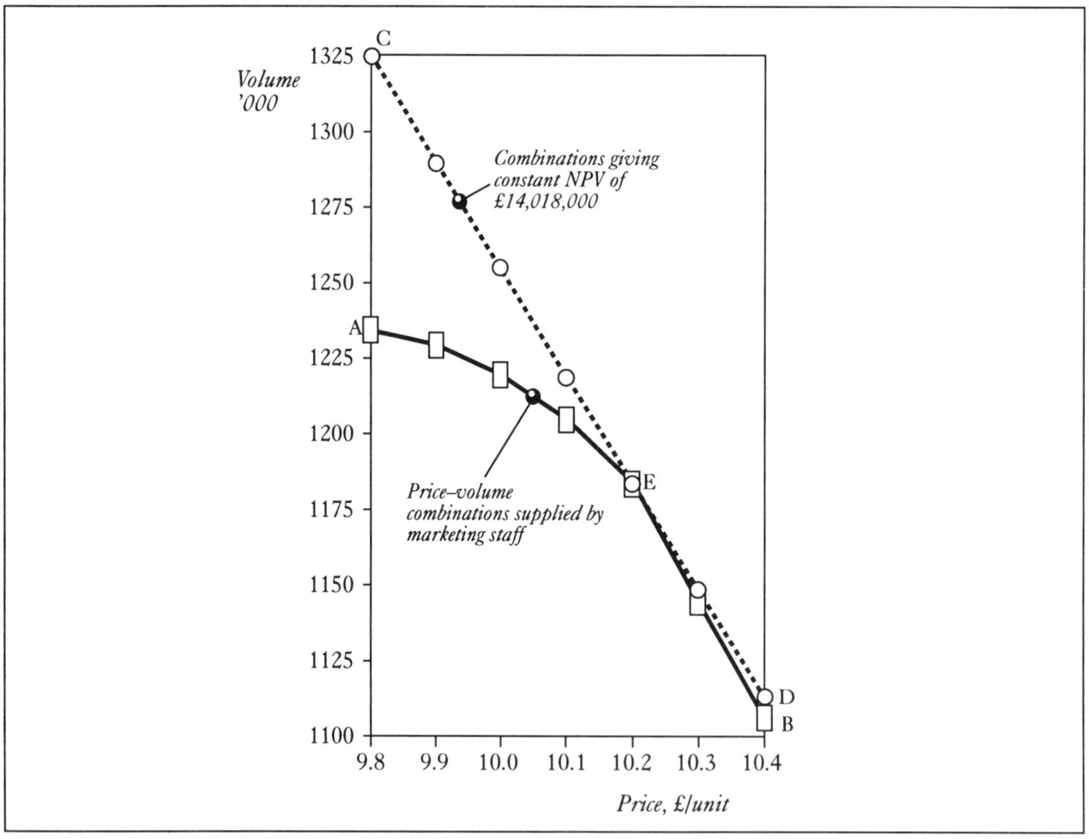

As indicated, Table 2 presents the calculation of the optimal pricing policy from among those considered under the high media strategy. Similarly Tables 1, 3 and 4 present the calculation of optimal pricing policies under each of the alternative media strategies.

It can be seen that the preferred strategy is that of low media advertising combined with foregoing the premium and setting a price of £9.8 from year 1 onwards (as in Table 3).

10.4 Concluding remarks

In the event, Stapylton's selected strategy was implemented and, although their media campaign did not start until three months after the introduction of Lynnfields' new-size package, details of its new policy were available to retail customers before orders would need to be placed for the new-size packages. This enabled Stapylton to offset the impact of Lynnfields' policy change and the marketing plans were met. Stapylton has continued to increase its share of the branded market at Lynnfields' expense. Not surprisingly, Lynnfields has resorted to other lines of attack. As envisaged when examining the data produced to estimate Lynnfields' operating costs, Lynnfields has tried to utilise the lower basic prime cost of their product to enable them to offer discounts to retailers. Most recently it has undertaken development of its own product range to include one which, it is claimed, will match, if not outperform, Stapylton's qualitative advantage in ease of use. Stapylton's management team are gathered again to consider their reaction.

10.5 Questions

1. Management accounting texts place significant emphasis on information relating to internal activities. Evaluate the importance of external information in this case, identifying the means adopted on a regular basis by Stapylton and suggesting further sources.

2. Discuss the suitability of the options identified by the company in response to an external competitive threat.

3. Examine the data utilised in assessing the various options, identifying the source of each element.

4. 'My problem, as the accountant, was to pin down the marketing man to having to quantify the various options. Accounting played the right part and made them quantify.'

   Do you agree with this statement? Examine the accountant's role in quantifying options, including the means by which he 'made them quantify' and his approach to analysing the results.

11 Edford

11.1 Synopsis

Edford is a long-established and well-known manufacturer in the durable goods market, principally the consumer durable goods sector. It is one of three or four companies which dominate the market, each of which aims to be the market leader.

In many respects it has had a history typical of many UK manufacturing companies in that, until recently, investment had been neglected, and management systems were out of date and inadequate. Since its acquisition a few years ago by a multinational company outside the UK, substantial new investment has been made, and amongst other changes a new senior accounting team has been brought in.

One of their immediate tasks, beyond guiding the investment programme, was a review and subsequent rapid up-date of the management accounting system. Previously the information supplied by the system had little value to management, particularly in view of the highly competitive nature of the final product market.

More recently, the accountants reached the conclusion that even the up-date of the management accounting system was not completely satisfactory in supplying information vital to running the business. They embarked on an enquiry which has led to the investigation of the potential for activity based costing (ABC) to be adopted in the company.

The case describes the company background, the nature of its management accounting system and how the investigation of the potential of ABC is being conducted.

11.2 Background

The company

The company was established over 100 years ago. It was taken over in the 1970s by a UK conglomerate and sold again in 1987 to a large organisation with headquarters in Europe (outside the UK). A new senior accounting team has joined the company since 1987.

The company was formerly located on two sites. Marketing was originally based in London, but this site has now been closed, with most of the activity transferred to the Midlands and located on the same site as manufacturing. The Midlands unit, which is at the centre of this study, is now regarded as a fully integrated manufacturing and marketing unit. It also carries a full range of spares, a unique feature amongst the Division's UK companies which belong to this Group.

The product range comprises space heaters, with the major part of the range dominated by one type.

A high proportion is marketed through a single retail outlet. There is no national pricing of products. The principal customer uses a standard mark-up on the manufacturer's price, but displays the price to its customers generally as a discount on a recommended price. Other retail outlets follow a similar pattern in setting customer prices.

These retail outlets also add their own mark-ups to the final customer service team, trained by the company, but other final customers are serviced directly by the company's own service department. It is also worth noting that extensive stocks of spares of decorative 'add-ons' which have been superseded in design are not kept, so that if a customer wishes to replace a single damaged item it may be necessary to buy a whole new set in order to maintain the appearance of the product.

In order to reach a profitable position, the company needs to obtain a market share of between a fifth to a quarter of the total of a very competitive market. The break-even point on its operation is correspondingly high.

Substantial investment in new plant and equipment has taken place in the last few years, with the result that the company has been able to maintain the same volume of output with a 30 per cent reduction in direct labour. There is a significant learning curve effect when new products are introduced into the range and also, to a lesser extent, when face-lifts are given to existing products.

11.3 Case details

The costing system

This is about seventeen years old, though it has recently (1987) undergone significant change. Prior to 1987, the manufacturing unit was treated as a single cost centre with overhead recovered to products via a blanket overhead rate based on direct labour costs.

Costs were built up as follows:

- Direct material – a standard quantity, with a contingency (2 per cent) for scrap and a 5 per cent cost contingency for inflation and stock losses.
- Direct labour/manufacturing overhead – as stated, a single overhead recovery rate on direct labour cost, though six different labour grades were identified.
- Certain manufacturing-related overhead was separately identified, including R & D, buying, and manufacturing administration, and was recovered to product using the concept of a 'standard product equivalent'. Individual products were measured by means of a judgement as to their 'complexity' in relation to this standard, and these costs were absorbed according to relative complexity.
- Sales, marketing and distribution cost was not added to product cost – full absorption costing was taken to works cost level only. This leaves a contribution to 'fixed' commercial overheads.

No recording of work in progress took place. Stocktaking was carried out twice a year, once for cost control and once for the annual accounts. Labour cost was expensed each month.

Although the direct labour content of work was said to be based on a 'standard' input, it was really an inaccurate estimate, not supported by proper work or method study.

Even the direct material content of products, similarly expressed as a standard, did not really deserve that description in that the 'standard' tended to remain the same each year, so changes taking place in a product's original specification would not be followed by an up-date of material standards.

The changes made to the system in 1988 were quite extensive.

In the first place, 'standard costs' were re-established on a more thorough basis:

- Product material requirements have been audited three or four times to provide a standard bill of materials, which is regarded as 98 per cent accurate. Material prices are set by the buying office and remain valid for the budget year. Allowance is made for inflation, but 'tasks' are set for the buying office, engineers, etc., with the aim of obtaining a reduction in the basic price. For example, a supplier may be given sole supplier status, with a resulting increase in order volume; in return, a reduction in unit supply price could be negotiated.

- Operation routeings with time-studied timings have been introduced for the whole product range. Synthetics are also used in establishing standards as products change, since 'new' products are not always totally new but modifications to existing products.
- Two years ago, manufacture was divided into four cost centres:

1. Press shop – (from coil steel) incorporating guillotine, blanking, welding.
2. Finishing – degreasing, and two finishing processes: painting, enamelling (there is a proposal to split the latter into separate cost centres at a later date).
3. Controls – gas taps (from brass bar), pipework.
4. Final assembly – there are nine assembly lines, some of which run at automatic speeds.

In the first three centres, there are individual cost rates for labour and for recovery of overhead, the latter based on machine hours. The assembly line overhead recovery is based on a weighted average of direct labour cost.

Standards, both physical and cost, are much more accurate than they were previously. Standard bills of materials have been developed, which also facilitate the rapid up-date of standards following specification changes. Problems do remain, though:

- There are large perceived differences in the costs of the two finishing processes. Although this is widely acknowledged, it is a problem which has not yet been properly examined. It is known that the process cost of one of the processes is much higher than the other although the process cycle time is much the same; the more expensive process incurs much heavier expense in usage of energy and water.
- Distribution of overhead to the four cost centres is still largely based on traditional arithmetical allocations and apportionments. For example, maintenance is simply divided equally amongst the four cost centres. New computing software has been introduced which has improved the ability to identify cost to cost centres via improved expense codings. The computer system remains, however, predominantly directed towards financial reporting.

Altogether, a better identification of cost with product is still needed.

- Research and development has traditionally been separate from manufacture, and R & D engineers had little notion of the cost consequences of their proposed designs once these were brought into manufacture.
- Marketing also did not have a sound product cost base for planning its own operations, nor does it have a clear idea of the way it uses its own resources and hence their ultimate cost impact on products.

Plant and product

During the last few years, substantial investment in new plant, equipment and tooling (most tooling is nowadays bought in) has taken place which has increased the element of automation in the manufacturing process as well as the quality of production.

Along with other organisational improvements, this has helped bring about a big improvement in the final product quality. Today, about 88 per cent of products coming off the final assembly track are 'right first time', whereas previously this had been as low as 8 per cent, resulting in a very high proportion of appliances coming from assembly in an incomplete state.

Internal inspection and quality control has been greatly improved recently, with the objective of zero defects in internal manufacture.

Certain components are bought in, for example, switches, timers, wiring harnesses, decorative additions, thermostats. Quality control for these items is related so far as possible to inspection of the systems of control operated by the suppliers at their own plants. Once again, the aim is a 'zero-base inspection', but not all suppliers are able to achieve this target and therefore are subject to increasing levels of inspection (up to 100 per cent) at Goods Inward, depending on their quality rating.

Internally, the company regards itself primarily as a 'metal basher', but the final products are to a significant extent fashion goods: up to 40 per cent of business each year can be in face-lifted products. Manufacture is adopting a common construction so far as possible, so that essentially products have the same chassis and are differentiated (as fashion goods) by different add-on features.

Other changes

An important organisational change (apart from the 'integrated site') has been the introduction of project teams. Previous poor liaison between design, manufacture and marketing is being tackled by the creation of multi-disciplinary project teams, with each team containing, besides the Divisional Directors, representatives from sales, marketing, production, finance and R & D. Overall, the general philosophy is to take the marketing-driven product design and ensure it is also a design capable of efficient and cost-effective manufacture.

Investigating activity based costing (ABC)

For reasons referred to above, the new accounting team considered that the improvements to the cost/management accounting system introduced since 1987 were still not able to provide the required level of detail and accuracy in the way cost was generated and related to products. It was felt that the real cost drivers were not properly understood at various points in the organisation and that this situation could lead to significant distortions in the costing of activities, departments and products. It was necessary to make direct investigation of how cost was incurred rather than relying on traditional allocations and apportionments. A good example of how views have been changed already by an as yet incomplete study of the supply of spares is that spares are no longer regarded as a 'nice little earner' (see 'The case of spares').

In the first place, the accounting team has had to try to obtain the commitment of departments throughout the company to the carrying out of the ABC investigation. It has been less successful in obtaining this in manufacturing (although it is thought this is the most important area in the benefits it will yield) than in sales and marketing. Manufacturing management is thought to be too busy 'firefighting'. It was also considered that the accountants had a better 'credibility' with marketing than manufacturing, which ultimately was a major influencing factor in the final decision to carry out the first study in marketing.

Consultants have been used for a first-stage investigation in sales and marketing. In deciding which consultants to use, the company's own auditors were specifically excluded. It is hoped, given success, that the results will eventually persuade manufacturing (including buying) to co-operate with the extension of the exercise to the whole company. Lessons will have been learned also as to how to conduct the exercise, thus easing the task of dealing with the more complex case of manufacture but minimising the need to use consultants.

The investigation has commenced with the analysis of distribution, sales, marketing and after-sales activities to products, product groups, customers, regions. Currently there is approximately £5½m of cost incurred by these functions which is not allocated to product groups, etc. In addition, the controllership function is also being analysed to determine the realistic split of its cost between marketing and manufacture.

Some details of the product range will give an idea of the complexity of the exercise. There are:

- Fifteen basic models, each differentiated by size, output, voltage, fuel types and finished in three colours.
- Three other types of heater, again with three colours, two voltages and two fuel types.

Some 6,500 component parts are stocked, of which about one-third relate to appliances in current production.

ABC study procedure

An interview technique has been used, starting with the head of a function and proceeding down through the lower levels of management in the organisation.

The questions are basically the same at each stage:

to establish how a manager

- divides his/her time between different activities;
- expects his subordinates to divide their time between different activities.

A matrix of expenditure and allocation to function is developed from this. Attention then turns to identification of the cost drivers.

In relying mainly on the interview technique, it is necessary to guard against obtaining a picture emerging of what appears to be happening based (in the recollections of interviewees) primarily on what has happened in the last few days or weeks; time is required, probably a few months, to gain a view of an activity which is truly representative.

Many changes in the way costs are allocated are expected to be made. A simple example is that the costs identified with 'sales orders' are no longer to be allocated 'per order', but instead on the number of lines per order. On a more macro scale, significant differences in the costs of supplying and servicing the dominant customer relative to other customers are also showing up in a comparison of what they were previously thought to be. The administration of spares in relation to service, new appliances and inter-company business can also be analysed.

The case of spares

Partially as a result of the above, and partially through other internal exercises, the view of the supply of spares being a highly profitable operation has been completely changed.

Spares only represent 4 per cent of the volume of business, but with a gross contribution of around 59 per cent on standard cost, they were considered to contribute a useful amount to overall business profit. This view of spares coloured issues such as the design and commonality of parts and also how they are ultimately supplied when bought in.

The price of a spare part which is currently in production is based on standard cost, reviewed annually as part of the normal budgetary process. For non-current parts, i.e. parts relating to products which have reached the end of their life, stock is held at the landed cost (i.e. the current standard cost at that time) indexed by a factor for inflation for the number of years it has been held in stock. The ultimate selling price is calculated from the latter. One of their customers is a near monopoly buyer and can sometimes be difficult over accepting the resultant annual price increase.

Although spares generate only 4 per cent of the business of the company, they generate 85 per cent of the invoices raised.

The following illustrates the view of the profitability of the spares business prior to the ABC-type analysis:

	% Sales
Sales	100
Manufacturing standard cost of sales	41
Gross contribution	59
Less: allocation of site overheads:	
energy/utilities	3
rates, security, canteen	9
Net contribution	47

It was considered the net contribution provided an ample margin to cover other overhead which the accounting system could not identify to spares and which were thus largely allocated to sales and marketing. When these were finally analysed, the following emerged:

	% Sales
Net contribution	47
Less: Operational allocations	
Commercial	18
Warehouse/distribution	16
Finance/systems	17
Selling/admin.	4
Operating profit/(loss)	(7)

Far from being a 'nice little earner' spares sales as priced and currently supplied emerged as a loss maker!

It is also worth noting that as quality and reliability improve, the spares volume should see a decline.

11.4 Concluding remarks

The company is still experiencing the problems of not knowing how successful/efficient the various parts of the business are. Although it is close to being the market leader amongst its competitors, competition is severe and the break-even point high. As with many businesses today a high proportion of cost is short-term fixed, with direct labour cost not being a particularly important cost in itself. The accountants even regard direct material costs in the category of short-term fixed, since contracts for quantities and price are settled for several months ahead.

It has moved rapidly away from a seriously out-dated costing system, through to an improved system and on into the attempt to introduce and implement activity based costing. However, it has yet to demonstrate that ABC is worth the effort, although the initial exercise with spares has had a marked impact on opinion, at least within marketing. The accountants have yet to win buying/manufacturing over to the cause.

11.5 Questions

1. What might be considered the advantages and disadvantages of using consultants to carry out the initial investigation of the possible benefits from introducing activity based costing (ABC) and its eventual implementation?

2. Given a company which has a policy of leaving costs where they arise and not redistributing them to user departments, how could the case for ABC be argued?

3. Would it be easier to implement ABC in a company which has an up-to-date standard costing system as opposed to one without such a formal system?

4. Discuss the strategy followed by the accountants in seeking to introduce ABC into the company.

5. Suggest a programme to be followed covering the investigation and possible subsequent introduction of ABC into the manufacturing area of the company. What might be considered the main problems to be tackled?

12 Gatwick Components

12.1 Synopsis

Transfer pricing can be seen as the implicit result of organisation structure: the need to measure unit and managerial performance while motivating managers and enabling and encouraging group optional decision-making. This case concerns these conflicting pressures and the resultant behavioural issues.

The case relates in particular to one profit centre within a Division, manufacturing components largely for sales inter-Group. Set in the wider context of the Division as a whole with manufacturing units and customers throughout Europe, the case allows the exploration of a wide range of organisational, transfer pricing, performance measurement and behavioural-related problems. It raises the question of how a complex multinational could and should establish its organisation structure, the implications for transfer pricing and performance measurement. The international dimension overlays these considerations as an added complexity to an already multifaceted position.

No element of the case can be considered completely in isolation. As is normal in practice, every facet of the situation must be considered and a balanced judgement made – in the interests of the Group as a whole, or perhaps of its parts! Behavioural considerations are inevitably inherent in any 'solution' to the case.

12.2 Background

The situation

Gatwick Components, aero component manufacturers, is one of six 'Product Divisions' within the Heathrow Group. This Product Division is itself organised into four divisions, UK, Europe, USA and International. Each of the four divisions sell two major products within their geographical area.

The UK division is organised into five companies.

1. Elmdon specialises in the manufacture and sale of Product A to the aerospace industry.
2. Luton manufactures and sells Product B to similar customers.
3. Bristol sells the same product types to other industries.
4. Stanstead manufactures components for Elmdon, Luton, the USA Division and some external customers.
5. Farnborough is the Product Division's development company and is based in the UK.

The European Division has a similar structure to that in the UK except that it has more than one manufacturing and selling company for each product, each trading geographically in the major European countries, i.e. the European equivalent of the UK Division's Elmden, Luton, Bristol and Stanstead. Each have several sites throughout Europe, typically in France, Germany and Italy.

Organisation control

It is Heathrow Group policy to treat all operational companies as budgeted profit/investment centres. Thus each is expected to meet its budgeted levels of profit related to sales and capital employed. Budgets are agreed by divisions and subsequently at Group head office. Actual performance is compared against budget periodically (on a 4, 4 and 5 week basis). Periodic results are not consolidated at any stage in the organisational hierarchy and are relayed directly to Group and Product Division head offices.

Stanstead was until recently a profit centre within the Components Division of Heathrow. However, following a reduction in Stanstead's sales to other Production Divisions, the unit had become a production unit for Gatwick's operating units and for Elmdon in particular. Some sales were still made to other Divisions. In many respects it might have been logical to establish Stanstead as a cost centre within the Elmdon Company: Group ethos, however, and the history of Stanstead as an independent profit centre within another division made such a change politically sensitive: 'We are in a different business, with different customers and different problems,' was the view of Stanstead's Financial Director. Gatwick's management, however, tended to view Stanstead for their internal control purposes more as being a part of the user product companies, recognising their performances were integral with them.

Managerial performance measurement

The 'performance' of all management staff was reviewed annually by their immediate superior. The review included performance criteria of achievement against target or budget in a wide range of performance measures including, where appropriate, ROCE (the principal measure) expressed in historic terms, working capital levels expressed as a percentage of the last three months' sales, and the sales to capital employed ratio (and thereby the profit to sales ratio). This written report (plus a one-to-one interview) was the cornerstone of Group personnel policy as a basis for motivation, promotional assessments and salary reviews. It was not normally relayed to Group Personnel, being held within the division in which the manager is working.

12.3 Case details

The market

Products A and B are sold to the aerospace industry. Sales in Europe and the UK were negotiated by a small sales team working on behalf of Gatwick Components as a whole from their sales and marketing office in Germany. Negotiations were conducted in this manner as many customers were themselves manufacturing on a similar international/European basis. Sales made were generally supplied by the operating company nearest to the required delivery point: thus a sale for delivery to Germany was likely to be supplied by the producing company in Germany. However, this practice could be altered for the benefit of the whole, should, for example, one operating company be either very short of work or in an over-capacity situation. In some cases, a particular order may be split between two operating units to provide the customer with a dual source facility. It should be remembered that the above sales were of major significance in size, taking perhaps two years or more to negotiate. However, once the order was obtained, it could be expected to pertain for several years, usually the duration/life of the aircraft concerned – and spares demand thereafter. In many respects, therefore, each operating company had a relatively high degree of certainty as to its sales volumes for the coming period, accepting the vagaries of governmental policies/military order and civil airline demand affecting significantly the absolute quantities demanded on a monthly and annual basis.

Stanstead

Stanstead, set up in 1954 as a separate company, was bought by Heathrow in 1966 and effectively served Elmdon, although there were also significant sales to Luton and Bristol and small volume sales to other parts of the Heathrow Group. Their machinery and tooling technology was constantly being updated both from their own developments and in particular those of Farnborough, the Division's development company, which had given the company a slight technological edge over many of their competitors. The company employed some 300 people. Stanstead purchased its raw materials from Deal Ltd, an operating company in another division of the Heathrow Group, and from major non-Group suppliers.

Purchases from Deal represented 20 per cent of Stanstead's total selling price. A further 20 per cent were also made from non-Group suppliers, mainly as a dual sourcing measure. As much as 85 per cent of Stanstead's sales were made to inter-Group companies: 60 per cent to Elmdon, 3 per cent to Luton (i.e. within the UK divisions) and 22 per cent to the US Division (within Gatwick Components but external to the UK division). The remaining 15 per cent of sales were made to customers outside the Group, being different types of components and using different technology to that used for intra-Group customers.

Group inter-company trading policy

It was the policy of the Heathrow Group that, as a general rule, purchases and sales shall be made from and to intra-Group companies in preference to any outside purchaser or supplier, i.e. there was a requirement on the buyer to buy internally if a source existed and for a seller to sell internally if a demand existed. However, if the seller was unable to match the market price, the buyer had the prima facie right to seek an outside source, except in the case of major transactions when the Group's overall interests were expected to override those of an individual unit.

It was Group policy that inter-company trading be at a market price if known, although negotiations around this level were acceptable. Where the market price was not known, prices were to be agreed by 'arm's-length negotiations' with a view to approximating to a market price, i.e. hopefully at the level which gives the supplier a recovery of his total costs and a profit margin. Should negotiations fail to produce an agreed price, there were provisions for decisions to be made at the next higher stage in the organisational hierarchy, i.e. for companies within a Division, the decision will be made at Division Head Office, and for disagreements between Divisions at Product Division Head Office, etc. However, it was not anticipated that this facility would be required very often, as amicable agreements were expected to pertain in the majority of cases.

Stanstead's transfer prices

The impacts on Stanstead of the application of Group policies were that :

1. Purchases of steel were made from Deal (an intra-Group company albeit in another product division of the Group), although similar volumes were purchased from non-Group suppliers as a dual sourcing precaution. These inter-company purchases were priced at the perceived market price which, apart from the price of purchases made from the non-Group suppliers, was relatively easy to ascertain.
2. Sales to companies within the UK Division were made at a negotiated price as a market price did not exist. No similar product existed within the UK, and even if it had it would have been unlikely that the price of this would have been readily available. Similar, though not identical, products were produced within the European Division and by other manufacturers in Europe. However, such a market price would not be considered a fair basis for pricing due to the products not being identical and also problems associated with setting a 'fair' international currency translation rate. As far as possible, these negotiations were conducted on an 'arm's-length' basis. The buyers (Elmdon and Luton) were unaware of Stanstead's product costs.

Similarly, Stanstead was not aware of the final products' profitability (although as members of the same Division, each was aware of Group policy and each other's overall profitability). The process was described as being with 'cards held fairly close to the chest'.

3. Sales to the US Division were made at a price which approximated to the market price of similar, though not as high quality, products available within the USA. There was no Group production facility equivalent of Stanstead within the USA Division.

Improvements in Stanstead's technology

Gatwick Component's development company (Farnborough), managed by an ex-Managing Director of Stanstead, designed and developed a new tooling technology. This enabled Stanstead and their European Division equivalents to produce a product of such quality that further operations, previously undertaken by Elmdon and Luton before incorporation in the final product, were no longer necessary. Thus, Elmdon and Luton could reduce their overall operating costs.

The investment in new tooling technology at Stanstead, specifically for intra-Group products, required substantial capital expenditures. As the capacity was attributable solely to Group sales, a re-evaluation of product standard costs and transfer prices was necessary. Some older technology facilities were retained for the servicing of work for non-Group companies, although the volume of this business had contracted substantially to only 15 per cent of total sales. Nevertheless, Stanstead was operating at about 70–80 per cent of their present maximum capacity, which was considered to be near full practical operating capacity on an on-going basis.

Elmdon and Luton profitability

Gatwick Components operated in a highly competitive environment on an international basis. Like other UK component manufacturers, sales volumes had contracted very substantially from the heyday of the British aerospace industry and, it was believed, had levelled out, although in comparison with their American competitors, their business was for relatively small volumes of a wider variety of product specifications. Due mainly to the lower sales volumes, Gatwick's profitability was reduced. Elmdon's management claimed that part of the reduced profitability was because they were buying from Stanstead instead of on the open market, although no identical component produced to such close tolerances was readily available. Envious eyes were made at Stanstead, who were producing a profit percent to sales of about 9 per cent. However, purchases from Stanstead represented only 16 per cent of Elmdon's costs and, therefore, a reduction in the transfer price would be unlikely to make a significant difference in Elmdon's profitability if viewed in percentage terms.

Imposition of a transfer price

The management to the UK Division was aware that the attitude to prices from Stanstead by other divisional companies could be detrimental to long-term performance and wanted to concentrate operational management's attentions on improving their competitiveness, finding economies, improving marketing, etc. Elmdon felt able to blame part of their low profitability on what they claimed were the high prices charged by Stanstead although this represented only a small percentage of their total costs. This, Gatwick's management believed, effectively deflected the management of Elmdon from the real problems.

In order to eliminate this attitude and concentrate management's attention on other economies, Divisional management decided to impose a 'below market' price upon the transfers from Stanstead to other UK intra-Group companies; in fact, to reduce the prices by about 6 per cent, anticipating the cost savings which would come from the anticipated capital investment at Stanstead necessary to implement the new technology. 'The idea of the change was to remove an emotional barrier – to give the Elmdon management less opportunity to say 'we are being screwed' and, therefore, be better able to concentrate on other areas – to try to economise, etc.'

This decision was taken 'in the best interest of the Division as a whole', although Divisional management believed that it was probably unfair to Stanstead. However, the end-users were the sellers in the market, while Stanstead were relatively small in relation to the scale of Gatwick's operations.

12.4 *Concluding remarks*

The financial effect on Elmdon and Stanstead

As indicated earlier, the true financial impact upon the Divisional end-user companies was relatively small: an average of 6 per cent of 16 per cent is still only 1 per cent of Elmdon's costs, although on a turnover of £60 million the saving represented nearly £600,000 of cost reduction.

The financial impact on Stanstead, however, was to reduce their profit percentage of sales from 9 per cent to 3 per cent before interest charges, well below the divisional and group yardsticks for financial performance, especially in view of the recent capital expenditures having been originally justified on different assumptions of transfer prices.

For these reasons, at Divisional level, the returns of the two companies were looked at in total.

The effect of the transfer price imposition

The decision to impose an 'artificial' transfer price was taken for behavioural reasons, albeit with a view to an improvement in financial performance in the longer term. It was impossible to be precise in the assessment of the decision in retrospect, as many other factors may have affected the position. Divisional management believe, however, that the Elmdon management were 'now far more competitive and efficient – they have retained business against fierce competition, cut prices and been forced to become more efficient. They are making reasonable profits at the same volume with 400 to 500 less people.'

When the price reductions were first proposed, there was a general acceptance at Stanstead that their fate was tied in with that of the end-user companies: that if they failed, then so too would they. To lessen the impact on Stanstead's profitability, ways of reducing their costs were discussed, leading ultimately to the sanction to acquire further new technology.

Although they had been assured that the reasons for their reduced margins would not be forgotten when they were assessed individually or as a profit centre, whether by Division or by Group, Stanstead's management now lost no opportunity in reminding the hierarchy that their performance had been affected by factors beyond their control. Divisional management had promised to 'ease the transfer price back to a normal and fair level' over the next few years. Stanstead management pointed out, however, that 'supplies to Elmdon have been maintained at very low prices throughout the recent difficult trading period'. However, while Elmdon margins were now considerably improved, little attempt had been made to improve Stanstead's prices to them. 'We went for a 3 per cent increase last year but only got 2½ per cent. Effectively they impose it on us. The Elmdon suggestion "that there is a low-price competition waiting to step in" is the only justification given which, while being consistent with a market price policy, is not taken seriously by the Stanstead management.'

In spite of this, Stanstead believe that there is a high degree of divisional loyalty as 'Elmdon makes positive efforts to put work Stanstead's way, even if the price is a little higher'.

12.5 Questions

1. Gatwick Components has four divisions – UK, Europe, USA and International, each selling two major product groups within their geographical area.

(a) What are the potential objectives, strengths and weaknesses of the existing organisation structure?
(b) Suggest two alternative organisation structures, and their relative advantages and disadvantages in relation to the existing structure.

2. Gatwick Components has four divisions – UK, Europe, USA and International, each selling two major products within their geographical area. What bases would you recommend for the performance evaluation of the four divisions, and why? What drawbacks might there be to the methods you have adopted?

3. Evaluate the methods and structure of the annual management performance measurement review for management staff in the company. In what respects, and for what reasons, would you want to change the appraisal system used by the company? What might be the implications of adopting the system you propose?

4. What controls, and for what purposes, would you place on Gatwick Components' sales team? How should their performance be measured?

5. The UK and Europe's operating units have similar production capabilities in that they specialise in the manufacture of product group A or B and/or components for these product groups. Gatwick's management would no doubt like to compare these units' relative performances. Why might they wish to do so? Why might any comparison be invidious? If it was decided that each unit should be compared, consider what bases might be adopted that would be 'as fair as possible'.

6. Identify the transfer pricing policy within the Group. What are the potential strengths and weaknesses of this approach? In what respects and for what purposes would you recommend any changes in this policy, if you were in a position to enforce a change?

7. In the light of the actions taken by the UK Division's management to impose a transfer price on transfers from Stanstead to Elmdon, consider the likely shorter- and longer-term behavioural impacts on the management of Stanstead, Elmdon and the UK Division.